RACE AND FAMILY IN THE COLONIAL SOUTH

Race and Family
in the Colonial South

Essays by
Thad W. Tate
Daniel Blake Smith
Philip Morgan
Russell R. Menard
Patricia Galloway
Robert Middlekauff

Edited by
Winthrop D. Jordan
and
Sheila L. Skemp

UNIVERSITY PRESS OF MISSISSIPPI
Jackson and London

Library of Cataloging-in-Publication Data

Race and family in the Colonial South.

Papers from the 12th Annual Porter L. Fortune, Jr.
Chancellor's Symposium in Southern History; published
under the auspices of the Center for the Study of
Southern Culture, University of Mississippi.
Includes bibliographies and index.
1. Slavery—Southern States—Congresses. 2. Slave
labor—Southern States—Congresses. 3. Southern States
—Race relations—Congresses. 4. Family—Southern
States—History—19th century—Congresses. I. Tate,
Thad W. II. Jordan, Winthrop D. III. Skemp, Sheila L.
IV. Chancellor Porter L. Fortune, Jr., Symposium on
Southern Culture (12th : 1986 : University of
Mississippi) V. University of Mississippi center for
the Study of Southern Culture.

Library of Congress Cataloging-in-Publication Data

E441.R26 1987   975'.03   87-23157
ISBN 0-87805-333-6
ISBN 0-87805-334-4 (pbk.)

This volume has been sponsored by the
Center for the Study of Southern Culture
at the University of Mississippi.

The paper in this book meets the guidelines for permanence and
durability of the Committee on Production Guidelines for Book
Longevity of the Council on Library Resources.

British Library Cataloguing-in-Publication data is available.

Contents

Acknowledgements

This volume reflects the 1986 proceedings at the twelfth annual Chancellor's Symposium in Southern History at the University of Mississippi. The first of these symposia was held in 1975 on the subject of slavery, at a time when that topic was downright guaranteed to make everyone at Ole Miss and indeed in the entire state feel very, very uncomfortable. Nonetheless, or perhaps therefore, that occasion brought together an astonishingly distinguished collection of scholars. For his courage in sponsoring this first and later, similar gatherings on an annual basis, these symposia have since been named in honor of then Chancellor Porter L. Fortune, Jr.

This collection focuses on "the colonial South" at a time in the seventeenth and eighteenth centuries, prior to the American Revolution, when "The South" may not even have existed, and hence probably should not even be capitalized. It deals with the structures of southern families, the lives of slaves and slaveowners, the development of the institution of slavery in its least accidental form in South Carolina, and Indian-White relations in colonial French "Louisiana."

While organizing these proceedings, we were helped by many people, all of whom are to blame for every failing and their spouses thanked. Most especially, Dr. Cora Norman and the staff and members of the Mississippi Committee for the Humanities provided substantial time and money which made the conference possible. We are very grateful for their doing so. We wish also to thank several supportive members of this University's administration: Chancellor Gerald Turner, Vice-Chancellor Morris Marx, and Dean Dale Abadie.

In our experience it is rare to have people come forward after a session to say how much they liked the public's questions that followed the paper. The questions from the floor were penetrating yet not hostile. We assign major responsibility for this magic

to several moderators: Susan Curry, Dennis Mitchell, Elizabeth
Nybakken, Bennie Reeves, and William Winter. In addition, Roy
Hudson of Mississippi Valley State University gave the con-
ference unusually effective support.

Many staff and faculty members in the Department of History
contributed to the proceedings and hence this volume. We select
several names out of gratitude: Ann Abadie (of the Center for the
Study of Southern Culture), Dale Abadie, Charles Eagles, Joanne
Hawks, Frederick E. Laurenzo, Harry Owens, Kees Gispen,
David Sansing, Charles Wilson, Robert Haws, Amanda Cooke,
Sara Dixon, Fredonia Hairston, Wanda Holly, Susan Pettis,
Neysa Rodriguez, and, behind the financial curtain, Ruby Robin-
son and Richard Douglas. We thank all.

Introduction

Until recently, at least, most historians of this nation have assumed that the American "South" has been the most distinctive region of the United States. There have been, of course, from time to time, some testy naysayers, those who lay claims for the Middle West, the Far Northwest, Texas and California (each sections of their own), Appalachia and New England, not to mention the several boroughs of New York City. And: the Sun Belt and the Rust Belt, the Middle Border, the Mountain Frontier, and the Eastern and the Middle States, not to mention the Old Southwest, now recently renamed the Mid-South. All these designations seem to have meaning. They designate, or at least pertain to, large and unitary expanses of geographical territory. These designations have specific spacial referents, with strong social attributes implied. There exist, however, other ways of denominating the land, ones where social components seem to outweigh the spacial—an environment where space seems less pertinent than social quality—as with the Inner City, Main Street, and the Crabgrass Frontier.

This intimate relationship between social and physical environments is variously but almost instinctively understood by human beings. Often it serves as the first link between two or several speakers of radically different languages when they chance or are forced to communicate verbally on their own. When they meet they start pointing. In this case the arm movements of anthropoid apes, London bobbies, and professors of history are remarkably similar when they are trying to communicate the concept of "where."

We raise these matters only because they have been so frequently applied to "the South." This region has commonly been regarded as the most distinctive part of the United States. Yet a glance at some physiographic maps immediately suggests that the South's distinciveness does not rest on any peculiar qualities of the land. After all, lowlying plains, partially split by lowlying mountains, bordered by a long and well-harbored seacoast, threaded with numerous rivers, possessing adequate but not overwhelming rainfall, and warm but not tropical temperatures— these attributes in themselves scarcely justify electing the region for candidacy in a pantheon of special separateness. Lest our thinking revert too fast to certain important staple crops, it ought to be borne in mind that tobacco can be and is grown in Connecticut and the same may be said of both rice and cotton in California.

While southern distinctiveness surely rests on social qualities more than on geography, we have often thought of these qualities without much reference to time. We tend to think of great plantations long before they existed, forgetting the appalling mortality and exploitation that characterized Virginia for well over half a century. We hear the rustle of crinoline when most people wore osnaburg or homespun. We think of the region as the Bible Belt when, if measured by any conceivable sort of social yardstick, it was the least Christian portion of the eastern seaboard of North America. We think we hear slaves talking English and white folks you-alling each other just all over the place.

If we read history backwards, of course, we can detect certain roots of southern distinctiveness prior to the era of the American Revolution. The pattern of settlement was, for most people of European background, more geographically scattered and less communal than in most other parts of the English New World. The rate of literacy among whites was higher than in the West Indian Islands, but lower than in the more northerly British-dominated colonies. The southern continental colonies had only one tiny urban center, a "city" (as it has been called) of about ten thousand people. The colonial "South" had much greater ethnic and linguistic diversity than the colonies to the northward. Actually the line between greater and lesser such differences was not Mason's and Dixon's, but a north-south one just east of the

Hudson River. In Pennsylvania, just north of Maryland, the first language of a great many people was German.

In the great sweeping geographical ark from Barbados to Maine, there were chattel slaves, mainly but not exclusively from western Africa. They came from a great many more different ethnic and linguistic groups than did the settlers from western Europe. For complicated economic and cultural reasons these people constituted, even as a group, a much smaller proportion of the population in the colonies from Pennsylvania northwards than in those further south. Yet it is important to bear in mind that the colony of New York had a proportion of slaves closer to North Carolina's than North Carolina's was to South Carolina's. And that Jamaica's proportion was double Virginia's. And indeed that in 1776 there were slaves in *every* British colony, including Massachusetts, Rhode Island, and other well-known slave emporia.

Still another factor added to the distinctiveness of the British southern continental colonies in North America. Like Quebec, Brazil, the West Indies and most parts of the new World, they lacked a balance of European women. "Sociologists tell us," that such a situation is likely to have certain consequences, that is to say that a low sex ratio leads to a low birth rate, miscegenation, poor family formation, and—here there seems to be a fork in the logical road—either a higher or lower status for this group of fewer women.

Perhaps the fork in the road is not in itself illogical. As one reads travel accounts by European visitors in the eighteenth century, one gains the sense that they (usually but not always male) were surprised by the ways in which these women in the American provinces were being regarded and treated. Disrespectfully degraded sometimes, but at others excessively adored. Possibly such views have a pedestal tone, yet in fact the essential ambivalence suggests eighteenth-rather than nineteenth-century sensibilities.

Because the colonial South is so difficult, perhaps impossible, to define, historians of the period have tended to concentrate their efforts on local or subregional studies. They talk of the Chesapeake, the deep South, the low country and back country, and even of the Old Southwest. They recognize that with the passing of time, differences in those regions blurred and connections between them solidified, but they also recognize that the South in the colonial period was more English than American and more American than southern.

Yet we can avoid reading history backwards by taking a different view of the problem. If we ask the question—""What did contemporaries think?"—a different picture emerges. As Professor John Alden showed some twenty-five years ago, Anglo-Americans first showed signs of consciousness about the existence of "the South" during the era of the American Revolution.[1] With the Stamp Act Congress and later the Continental Congresses, the thirteen continental colonies acquired a quasi-national forum and focus. It was then that John Adams and other delegates found themselves taken aback by regional distinctions within the generally distinguished gatherings.

As one might expect, regional differences emerged with even greater clarity when it came to discussing the very nature of the national government (if any), as well as specific measures that brought out and underscored differences in sectional interests. This was notably the case at the Constitutional Convention in Philadelphia. Once the Great Compromise on the House and Senate was hammered out, "It seemed now to be pretty well understood," James Madison quoted himself as saying on the floor, "that the real difference of interests lay, not between the large and small but between the N. and Southn. States. The institution of slavery and its consequences formed the line of discrimination. There were 5 states on the South, 8 on the Northn. side of this line."[2] It is not often noticed that Madison's count was a common one at the convention, for the delegates all seemed to have assumed that Delaware, as well as New York and

New Jersey, would soon pass gradual emancipation laws. Of course the latter two states did so within about fifteen years, but Delaware remained a slave state until the Civil War.[3] Was it therefore a "southern" state and Madison and other delegates therefore a group of incompetent social and political observers?

Here we have an historical fact so obvious that it is easily overlooked. The American Civil War was not a war between the South and the North, at least if the presence of slavery is taken as defining southernness. No matter how many individuals chose "the other side," the "border" slave states remained in the Union. In our experience teaching at a deep-South university, we have discovered that many undergraduates have to overcome a fair amount of surprise when they are so informed. Today we are placed in the anomalous position of saying, for example, that Maryland and Delaware are southern states but not "really" southern, or that parts of them are really southern and that parts of them are not. From Jackson, Mississippi, Baltimore looks like a northern city; from Boston, it looks very southern.

Another fact that has been even more neglected is that when we are talking about growing sectional consciousness in the late eighteenth century, we are talking about consciousness among whites, not blacks or Indians. For many years blacks had little reason to make sectional distinctions, though, of course, by the time of the Civil War they saw them as profoundly important. For blacks especially, of course, the existence of slavery was the touchstone. Yet in 1776 there were no free states, and in 1787 there were more slave states than free. For black people the North Star was a nineteenth-century phenomenon.

We might add one more caveat about regional consciousness at the close of the colonial period. The "five southern" states were sharply divided, along lines that foreshadowed the lines taken during secession and the Civil War. On the issue of the Atlantic slave trade the sectional division in 1787 was the Deep South versus the rest of the nation. The only reason the overseas slave trade was not banned outright in the Constitution was that the delegates from South Carolina and Georgia made clear their states would not ratify if the slave trade was not afforded some protection. Certainly the papers to follow make clear many of the reasons for this important crack in regional solidarity.

Yet to look at the original thirteen colonies cum states in isolation seems to us a mistake. It is for this reason that we have chosen to include the Old Southwest, the colony of French Louisiana (as then geographically defined.) Colonial history, as it is too-often taught to undergraduates and in American graduate schools, includes primarily and sometimes even exclusively the thirteen English continental colonies.

Had space permitted, we should have liked to broaden the scope of the symposium and this volume. The colonies located in the southern portions of eastern North America were in many ways unique. Most conspicuously they had a distinctive demographic history. Politically they were not so different from the West Indian islands, but they constituted the only area in the New World where slavery was at the same time firmly entrenched economically and self-sustaining demographically. As is now well known, the American South was the only plantation society (or societies) in the New World where the slave population reproduced itself. This is not a cold retrospective statistic. The conditions that led to this fact made some difference to the master classes and a very great deal to the slaves themselves.

Thad Tate set the stage for the conference. His paper discusses the efforts of historians in the past to define the South, and it calls upon future scholars to study the region on its own terms, from its own perspective. While Tate does not deny that the pre-Independence South was a land of rich diversity, he nevertheless insists that by the mid-eighteenth century, the area was becoming more of a recognizable and definable entity. As the backcountry was settled, two basic cultures began to emerge: one dominated by the Chesapeake, the other by South Carolina. And by the revolution, the way was prepared for the absorption into the region of the Old Southwest.

In his analysis of family formation in the seventeenth century, Daniel Blake Smith highlights some of the unique characteristics of southern family life, even while he emphasizes that the colonial family was vastly different from its counterpart in the Antebellum period. Family formation in the seventeenth century South was "a very difficult and often short-lived enterprise." Settlers had to face obstacles created by migration, a high mortality rate, isolation, and a formidable scarcity of women, making the stable nuclear family a phenomenon notable only by its absence. The unsettled frontier conditions of the new world resulted in loosened sexual mores, more independence for children of both sexes, and the development of what modern sociologists call a "blended family."

By the turn of the century, the immediate world of most Southerners had become more stable, and upper class parents, at least, could take a hand in guiding their childrens' lives and helping them prepare for a more certain future. But even lower class parents "instilled meaning and shaped values among their offspring." In either case, however, men more than women benefitted from this growing parental concern in an environment that was becoming increasingly patriarchal. This was "a society that launched sons and polished daughters."

Smith's description of the eighteenth-century family stresses the importance of family life in southern politics, as well as the increasing class divisions that characterized the region in the years before Independence. Still, he admits that the paucity of information renders it virtually impossible for historians to comprehend the inner workings of southern families, or to make any hard-and-fast generalizations about the institution, even in the mid-eighteenth century. But while he implies that real differences existed between northern and southern families, the data beg for comparative studies that will document and explain those differences more fully.

Philip Morgan's examination of three eighteenth-century slaveholders—Landon Carter of Virginia, Henry Laurens of

South Carolina, and Thomas Thistlewood of Jamaica—probes "in brief compass the range of possibilities" inherent in the eighteenth-century master-slave relationship. His analysis of one of the South's most important—and in the end, at least, most distinctive—social institutions is ideally suited to highlight the diversity and unity of the southern experience.

Morgan contends that eighteenth-century slavery operated within a system of patriarchy. Unlike the more sentimental paternalism of the nineteenth century, patriarchy was a harsh, austere code that stressed "order, authority, unswerving obedience." Its practitioners were quick to resort to violence if their authority was questioned. Slavery constituted a set of relationships based on personal domination, not on contractual bonds, and slaves themselves were not just property but were dependents who were in some sense part of the planter's household. Despite the basic similarities characterizing the slave experience, Morgan's examination of three slaveholders indicates that temporal, spatial, personal and social variations occurred throughout the South.

Russell Menard's concern with the institution of slavery has a different focus. His examination of the development and unique characteristics of slavery in the South Carolina lowcountry indicates, once again, the rich diversity of the southern experience. The concentration of slave ownership among the white inhabitants of South Carolina gave the colony its own peculiar flavor, and helped it to become, by the mid-eighteenth century, "a republic of slaveholders." Consequently, South Carolina seemed more nearly similar to the West Indies than to the Chesapeake colonies.

Menard traces the changes that occurred in South Carolina's slave population, as planters moved away from their early reliance on Africans from the West Indies and Native Americans, and toward a direct involvement with the West African slave trade. And he argues that supply and demand as well as the need for market stability, ultimately made African slaves the "victims of choice" for South Carolina's emerging ruling class. Menard's analysis of the inception of the colony's plantation society helps answer Tate's call for studies that approach the colonial South on its own merits without trying to force awkward parallels to the Antebellum South.

Patricia Galloway's concern is with two, often slighted, topics of interest to historians of the colonial South. Her description of Indian-French relations in eighteenth-century Louisiana provides a useful analysis of the interpenetration of cultures in the Southwest. The French colonials, whom she argues were imperialists but not racists, realized that their twin goals of conversion and economic exploitation would be made immeasurably easier and more palatable if they could converse in the language of the native Americans. The process, begun in a haphazard fashion by Cartier, was institutionalized by Pierre le Moyne d'Iberville, who sent young boys—cadets and cabinboys—to live with local groups of Native Americans. Because these lads were so young, they quickly learned more than the language of the host tribes. They adapted to and sympathized with the Native Americans, becoming, in many cases, individuals with one foot in each world, but not fully belonging to either. D'Iberville's policy was accomplished at the expense of the young men who were central to its implementation.

Galloway's study provides a useful corrective to the view that the colonial South was a world dominated by English whites and African blacks. The contributions of the French and Indians, as well as of the Spanish, were essential components of the development of southern culture.

Robert Middlekauff's rigorous critique of each of these papers helps place the contributions of the participants in perspective. In particular, his advocacy of comparative studies and his insistence that the colonial South must be seen in an imperial context, are especially worth attention. As he makes clear, local and regional studies must also continue; analyses of religion, education and politics in the South must be integrated with studies of race and family.

And historians must be willing to admit similiarities and common values that colonial southerners shared with their northern counterparts. We must not be too quick to perceive differences or establish dichotomies where none existed or where they were of relatively minor importance. We can leave the Civil War to the historians of the nineteenth century, focussing on a time when the South was as American, and as English, as it was southern. The South before it became the South.

RACE AND FAMILY IN THE COLONIAL SOUTH

Defining the Colonial South

THAD W. TATE

To refer to the American South evokes an image of a distinct geographic area but even more of a certain regional identity, even a distinctive culture. That southern consciousness finds its focus, however, in the nineteenth-century—in the antebellum era, the Civil War, and the years that followed. We sometimes speak almost as confidently, nevertheless, of a colonial South spanning the century and a half from colonization to the eve of the American Revolution. Yet any examination of scholarly historical writing on that earliest period of southern history brings one quickly to a realization that the "colonial South," in any sense of a collective entity embracing the seaboard southern colonies and possibly the territory of the Old Southwest, is an elusive term, a concept almost without a supporting historical literature.

Those historians who have written of that earlier South have for several reasons encountered unmistakable difficulties both in defining its territorial limits and the particular qualities and character that the region shared. Wesley Frank Craven caught the nub of the problem when he began the preface to his classic *Southern Colonies in the Seventeenth Century* by noting, "To write of the South when there was no South is a task not without difficulties."[1] There are few historians besides Craven who have made any effort at such a synthesis. Thomas J. Wertenbaker's now largely overlooked *Old South: The Founding of American Civilization*, Clarence Ver Steeg in his prefatory remarks to *Origins of a Southern Mosaic*, Allan Kulikoff most recently in his epilogue to *Tobacco and Slaves: The Development of Southern Cultures in the Chesapeake, 1680-1800*, are among the few examples.[2] The eighteenth-century volume of the standard multivolume history of the South issued by Louisiana State University Press remains uncompleted forty years after the series was launched, although

3

the currently assigned author, Peter Wood, has outlined a promising approach in a brief preliminary statement.[3] Aubrey Land's 1983 Southern Historical Association presidential address, "The American South: First Epiphanies," offers the most recent consideration of the problem of defining the colonial South, one which, however, finds the matter as perplexing as this essay does.[4] In effect, there is no major synthesis of the history of the colonial South, and at least one major southern historian, John Alden, in *The First South*, finds no clear consciousness of a southern identity or interest earlier than the American Revolution.[5]

Among these authors there is also no essential agreement on the geographical extent of the colonial South, though all but Alden agree it existed. Ver Steeg accepts the traditional conception that it comprised the five British seaboard colonies from Maryland southward, whereas Wood proposes to add the territory of the lower South from Alabama across the Old Southwest, enlarging the size and significance of the native American population of the region and adding small but culturally important French populations. This new definition with good reason seems likely to prevail.

In the final analysis historians, even those who define its geographic extent more narrowly, find the very diversity of the colonial South, the sharp differences in economy, social organization, and political systems, the overwhelming characteristic of the region. Ver Steeg comments perceptively, if briefly, on the problem, concluding that it does not beg the question of the character of the colonial South to say it is defined by "its quilt-like mosaic, identifiable enclaves that contribute a special quality to the whole."[6] Carl Bridenbaugh's *Myths and Realities: Three Societies of the Colonial South*, dealt with the contrasting social orders of the Chesapeake, the Carolina Lowcountry, and the Southern backcountry without attempting any integration of the three.[7] And Land concluded his address by observing that "the search for beginnings, for the earliest Souths, has disclosed diversity, distinctive societies neither well understood nor properly outlined until recent memory."[8]

Yet most of these historians, even Alden, seem to assume that collectively these diverse colonies or subregions provided important antecedents of the later South. These are conventionally perceived, as Alden suggests, as slavery, a distinctive farming system, a characteristic natural setting, and perhaps a temperament among its inhabitants that differed from that of the more northern colonies. It must be said, however, that such observations are more nearly derived from reading back into the colonial era commonly assumed features of the antebellum South that may have originated in some form in the southern colonies than by explicitly tracing the linkages forward from southern colonial life. This is understandable; yet colonial historians are also increasingly aware that such an important aspect of southern culture as, say, slavery had different characteristics in its formative years from those in the antebellum era and also took somewhat different forms in colonial Virginia and South Carolina, the two colonies with by far the greatest black population on the North American mainland. Land identified this hazard nicely when he remarked, "To impose the pattern of a full-blown culture on a primitive past creates a self-fulfilling prophecy of things to come."[9]

These problems are in some respects so formidable as to suggest that perhaps Ver Steeg's solution of simply accepting a mosaic-like colonial South does, despite his denial, beg the question, or at least argue that there was in truth no colonial South, only a diverse group of colonies who at some later point, as Alden argues, finally began to converge in their interests and develop a consciousness of their differences from other parts of the American nation.

Certainly, as the limited extent and problematical nature of a literature that seeks to synthesize colonial southern history might suggest, historians have concentrated upon investigations of individual colonies or one of the major subregions of the South.

Although the colonial southern colonies have over the long run
never attracted the kind of attention that Puritan New England
has received, and although colonial history of any kind was not a
major field of inquiry between the two World Wars, studies of
specific southern colonies or subregions have far outnumbered
the few efforts at synthesis that we have examined. The best
historiographical treatments of the colonial South, while attempting to identify some broad themes, generally record a body of
work that focuses on individual colonies.[10]

Insofar as historians of the southern colonies have been concerned with the broader implications of their work, they have
until very recently sought primarily to link the early South to
interpretations which applied to the entire British imperial world
or to general American national development far more than they
have attempted to discover the origins of a distinct regional
identity. At times, certainly in the more popular historical literature but also in some scholarly writing, one can even detect
assertions of the absolute primacy of the colonial South over other
colonial regions in its contributions to the nation—from the establishment of the first successful British colony within the region
to its having furnished a major share of the leadership in the
Revolution and the first years of the new nation.

This inclination toward a national rather than a regional orien-
tation persisted through the successive appearance over the first
half of the twentieth century of several major interpretive over-
views of the colonial era. Whatever differences adherents of one
school had with those of another, whether they emphasized the
long development of libertarian political institutions and values
transferred from England and transformed in America, the protective and nurturing shield of the British Empire, or more
sharply divided colonial politics in which democratic and popular
forces contended against imperial power and colonial elites, all
described a political process that culminated in the American
Revolution and all saw the southern colonies participating fully in
the creation of an American nation. However imperfectly united

the nation was in its beginnings, in the eyes of these early twentieth-century historians the southern colonies and states played their part in a generally nationalizing and liberalizing trend throughout the colonial era.

The immediate post-World War II era, in the late 1940s, through the 1950s and into the 1960s, marked a strong renewal of interest in the political history of the colonial and Revolutionary era and its origins. The inclination of many historians of that era to emphasize the ability and experience of late colonial political leadership, the extent of agreement on libertarian constitutional and political principles among politically conscious colonists, and, in some colonies, especially those of the South, the remarkable stability and confident authority of that leadership seemed to mark a return to an old so-called Whig view of Anglo-American history. It earned for the group the label of neo-Whigs, or sometimes consensus historians, for their denial that deep social and political divisions existed in the early American social and political order. Those terms are now ones of disapproval in a time of changed historical interests. Yet, it is sometimes overlooked by more recent critics of the history written in these years how much its practitioners sought to understand the social and cultural bases of colonial politics by probing the degree and manner in which leaders had to appear responsive to constituents and the extent to which social reality and political practices often coincided among the free population of the colonies.

It is scarcely too strong to say that the political history of the southern colonies was substantially rewritten in those years by historians such as Charles Sydnor, Jack Greene, Eugene Sirmans, Robert Weir, William Abbot, Wilcomb Washburn, and Richard M. Brown.[11] Relatively little of the work addressed the South collectively, apart from Greene's *Quest for Power*. It still treated individual colonies and did not argue for a distinctive South, but in some respects the political order of the South did tend in a common direction. With the late but successful conversion of Georgia to a royal colony, it was from Virginia south the only one

of the major British colonial areas on the North American mainland organized exclusively under Crown control. As John Murrin
has recently pointed out anew, the Southern mainland was also
the area that exhibited by the late colonial period the greatest
amount of internal harmony and absence of marked factionalism
among its leadership. [12] Although North Carolina—and the so-
called backcountry generally—did not fit this pattern very well,
at least some of the new work had even begun to qualify the
exceptionalism of the interior and to suggest that backcountry
dissidence came from property owners who sought fuller integration into the political and social systems of their colonies.
Whether these various attributes were interconnected in any
significant way was still, however, problematical. One still had to
look ahead to the contrast between the strength of Loyalism in
the lower South and the interior during the Revolution and its
comparative weakness in Tidewater and Piedmont Virginia, and
one still had to confront significant differences in the character of
politics in all four colonies.

More than a half century of rich and varied scholarship had on
the whole, succeeded, however, in demonstrating that within the
comparable patterns of regionalization and subregionalization
that characterized all the colonies of Britain's American empire
the South had shared, as the West Indies had not, in a process of
political maturation under common traditions of the colonial
experience and in a sufficient degree of social and cultural identity with the other mainland colonies to make possible the American Revolution and the establishment of the nation. It is a
parameter of southern history that ought not be forgotten. But
the historians of those years had not defined, and indeed had not
sought to define, a distinctive colonial South.

In the past two decades the writing and interpretation of early
American history, that of the southern colonies included, has
turned strongly in other directions, employing other methods,
including the quantitative methods of the social sciences and the
analytical processes of cultural anthropology, and addressed other

questions. We can point, for example, to a vast enrichment of black history in the first century of American slavery, with more attention to the flow of black migration and population growth; the varieties of acculturation that blacks experienced, both from contact with one another and from interaction with whites; or the actual working of slavery as a labor system rather than as a legal institution. In a somewhat comparable manner ethnohistorians have looked in fresh ways at the native American population of early America, treating more fully various Indian cultures, their intersection with European cultures, and their persistence against the pressures of commerce and colonization. Nor has the white colonial population escaped a similar scrutiny, by examination in greater depth of social structure and distribution of wealth, reemphasis on the extent to which white colonists formed an immigrant population of great ethnic diversity, and reconsideration of the extent to which colonial society and culture remained stubbornly traditional or was drastically transformed by the experience of colonizing a new world. If much of the new work is usually perceived—and no doubt correctly—as emphasizing social history, it is a broadly defined social history extending, among other things, to economic considerations, values and ideology, and material conditions of life. Despite the impatience of some social historians with the history of politics, much of the more recent work has also achieved a further refinement of early American political history, focusing even more on the intersection of society and politics and on the informal processes by which political systems often work.

In the case of the southern colonies, the emphasis upon social history has been greatest in the recent study of the Chesapeake region, at first for the seventeenth century but now extending into the eighteenth. Newer studies on the two Carolinas have generally had a more political or economic thrust, except for work on black history. Everywhere black history has, in fact, begun to receive major attention, as has that of Indian peoples of the Southeast. The southern interior, apart from a continuing interest in the Regulator movements, has, on the other hand, been slower to attract attention.

Yet, in the case of the colonial South, this more recent historical literature remains one that treats individual colonies and subregions much as the older work had done. Indeed it may reaffirm, even extend, that longstanding impression of great diversity, since the concentration of much of the recent social history on intensive studies of small populations in specific localities—a single county or community—encourages an even more localist perspective and accentuates very real differences among colonies and within a single colony.

In many respects, especially in its concern with broad social and cultural questions, the new work does, however, bring us closer to a careful examination of at least some of those features of southern life that have traditionally seemed to shape the strong regional identity of the nineteenth century—features such as race, the labor system, and plantation agriculture. And, even if the results should in some part confirm persistent subregional variations throughout the colonial era, we may at least trace those characteristic southern institutions as they grew historically from their earliest beginnings rather than looking back on them from the vantage point of their fullest development.

While it remains clear that strong racial feeling of whites toward blacks was present from the beginning of colonization, as noted especially in Winthrop Jordan's *White Over Black*,[13] and that lifetime slavery as a legal institution developed in the Chesapeake within the first century of settlement, we now understand that neither widespread employment of slavery nor a large-scale black presence became characteristic of Chesapeake society until almost the end of the seventeenth century. By that time the Chesapeake colonies had developed a plantation economy based on tobacco and a work force of white servants indentured for periods of a few years. The resultant social and economic order had passed well beyond Thomas Wertenbaker's vision of a yeoman-farmer democracy. From very early a small number of larger landowners had controlled a significant proportion of indentured labor, but even among that group the scale of agriculture was smaller than it would become in the next century. Nonetheless, the main outlines of a staple-crop, plantation economy and an unfree labor system had developed without any significant reliance on slavery.

At the end of the seventeenth century, beginning by the decade of the 1680's and gaining momentum in the first decades of the eighteenth, a vastly increased flow of black arrivals, most of whom were brought directly from Africa, began. In a few decades the combination of continuing importations and natural increase in Virginia established a black population that approached half of all those living in the Tidewater region and then began to expand into the new Piedmont sections of the colony. These new arrivals and their descendants were from the beginning held as slaves. Within a brief span their presence transformed the dominant Chesapeake labor system from the old base of white servant labor to black slave labor. This momentous shift would seem from the most recent and probing work on the subject to owe more to transatlantic focus—expanding supply of Africans, a stronger English presence in the trade, and the growing shortage of white labor—than to the preferences of Chesapeake colonists, although it was aided by the improved economic position of larger planters and an increasing survival rate that made a more expensive but more permanent labor force attractive.[14]

Any of several ramifications of this significant transition warrants fuller discussion than is possible here, but existing studies seem to suggest several significant effects of the development of slavery, apart from its late emergence without significant impetus from Chesapeake colonists themselves:

1. The large planters, those who already controlled the most servant labor and land, likewise acquired most of the earliest slaves and, even in a period of prolonged depression in the

tobacco economy, extended and consolidated their dominance of Chesapeake society and its economy.

2. With a growing increase in available slaves by the second quarter of the eighteenth century the number of lesser landowners who also acquired slaves increased dramatically, but the larger planters continued to own a disproportionate share—in sum, slaveholding became widely dispersed among landowners, although that change did not reduce the dominance of larger planters.

3. In the Chesapeake, however, even the largest planters tended to own fewer slaves than the great Carolina Lowcountry planters and tended, moreover, to divide their slaves into smaller work groups, frequently residing at different quarters of the plantation or on outlying lands. Slave communities were, therefore, smaller than older, more conventional views based on antebellum slavery have usually suggested.

4. Although slavery was the all but inevitable fate of blacks arriving after 1680 or of those born to slave mothers in Virginia and although slaves worked under harsh, demanding conditions, historians of colonial slavery still tend to emphasize elements of flexibility in the institution, features that were not yet as rigidly defined as they would become. They have pointed out how much slavery left the black population areas of autonomy in their personal lives—control of their family life, an acceptance by owners of slave marriages that were not recognized at law, some capacity to regulate work routines, independence in their social and religious life in the slave quarters, and a wide degree of clandestine but tacitly permitted contacts across neighboring plantations. There are, however, more recent signs of a renewed emphasis upon controls and restrictions on such autonomy, based on the uncompromising demands of slave labor and the inability to escape the fairly close scrutiny by whites that the small size and relative isolation of black communities on the quarters and plantations produced. Nevertheless, the development of a vigorous Afro-American culture, a varying amalgam of persistent African

inheritances with what had to be learned and adopted from the white Anglo-American world, remains an accepted feature of black life.[15]

The Chesapeake had developed, then, as a fully biracial society, and slavery had completed, although it had not initiated, the structure of the Chesapeake plantation system. It may be tempting to think that with perhaps some differences of scale and timing a similar pattern appeared in the Carolina Lowcountry. The earliest settlers in some cases brought slaves with them, yet for some decades slaveholding did not, as in early Virginia, dominate the labor system. The status and nature of social relationships with whites of those first black Carolinians also had much of the variety and flexibility of early race relations in Virginia. Yet the contrast between the two systems is marked.

The establishment of Carolina slavery was not as in the Chesapeake a gradual, slowly developing process, for slaves had come with the earliest arrivals, especially those brought by Barbadian planters, who relocated in Carolina with every intention of continuing the social and economic system with which they were already familiar. South Carolinians did not succeed, however, in finding a staple crop until rice took hold in the Lowcountry areas soon after the beginning of the eighteenth century, to be supplemented in time by indigo. Unlike tobacco, slaves were essential to rice cultivation from the beginning. Blacks from African rice-producing regions possessed the necessary knowledge of techniques that whites did not, and planters did not in any event think that white labor could stand up to the work of cultivating rice. Slavery and the staple were in this case more inextricably connected, and slavery took on different characteristics than in Virginia. Blacks worked in larger gangs under a different organization of work routines, and slave population in the Lowcountry itself soon far exceeded that of whites. Ownership was at the same time more concentrated among a small number of planters. Because of the larger number of black workers in a single work force and the greater infrequency with which they had contacts with whites—even white masters and their families often resided in Charleston for part of the year—Afro-American culture in Carolina retained a stronger African base. The Stono Rebellion of 1739 far exceeded in its force any examples of black restiveness or resistance in early Virginia. [16]

Despite a common labor base and major reliance on a staple crop raised for export, the two slave and plantation systems of the Chesapeake and the Lowcountry did not in important respects, then, much resemble one another. The recent work, if anything, may by its closer, more detailed examination of the two societies accentuate the differences. Some historians and geographers regard the Lowcountry as having shown a greater resemblance to the British West Indian colonies than to the Chesapeake. As their larger slaveholdings and long periods of absence from their plantations suggest, Carolina planters comprised a smaller, wealthier group. Their political power centered in the provincial government unlike the more dispersed Virginia elite, who had an equally strong base in their dominance of local county courts. Nor did Carolina planters share the growing of the principal staple with smaller landowners to the same extent as those of the Chesapeake. The Lowcountry possessed a major urban-commercial base in Charleston that the Chesapeake never developed. As South Carolina expanded, it did so by recruiting new groups of settlers of diverse European backgrounds whose settlements in the interior rested on different economic and social bases and were not easily integrated with the Lowcountry. The interior of the Chesapeake clearly differed in some respects, too, from its coastal Tidewater area, but in the Virginia Piedmont settlement spread in part from the older region, and with it slaveholding and tobacco cultivation. New counties were more rapidly absorbed into the political system by the full extension of county courts and representation in the Assembly.

Even so, Lowcountry and Tidewater Chesapeake societies may appear to have borne more resemblance to one another than either did to their interior regions, which comprised that third major subregion of the British colonies in the South, embracing substantial parts of North Carolina and Georgia as well as Virginia and South Carolina. The backcountry has, as already noted, received relatively little systematic attention, yet from what endures in older studies and from a few examples of significant new work, several characterists seem to stand out: (1) newness of settlement, which began no earlier than the 1720's and was still advancing as the Revolution approached; (2) a population composed of various European ethnic groups, chiefly German and Scotch Irish, as well as those of English stock; (3) similarly, a limited population of slaves, although slavery did exist in the region and was expanding rapidly in Piedmont Virginia; (4) an agriculture based on mixed farming and livestock, although with a sufficient commercial vision to constitute something more than subsistence agriculture alone; and (5) a settlement pattern that combined some flow of settlers through the older coastal regions of each colony with a significant southward thrust from Pennsylvania into the Valley of Virginia and ultimately across the entire region.

Earlier references to the two Carolina Regulator movements and to the sharply contrasting populations of Lowcountry and upland South Carolina suggests that relations between coast and interior were not always harmonious and that, not surprisingly in the light of how recently the interior had been settled, its political and social integration was hardly complete, though most nearly so in the case of the Virginia Piedmont.

The Regulator movements, the most visible expression of these tensions, continue to receive the greatest attention. As in the case of the study of the older coastal regions, emphasis has shifted away from the exclusively political toward an analysis of the social and economic conditions that helped shape the political contests. Certainly there are historians who are more convinced than ever that this evidence demonstrates a sharp cleavage along class lines and find the Regulation to have been a fundamentally radical movement, a challenge to an emerging South of planter elites and

slaveholding.[17] Yet, the stronger trend seems to be to interpret
the Regulator leadership as drawn from more substantial proper-
tyholders of the interior determined to end the domination of
local government in the North Carolina interior by corrupt, non-
resident officials appointed by the provincial authorities or in
South Carolina to secure the establishment of local courts and to
restrain disorder in the backcountry population.[18]

Political and economic integration had proceeded too far in
Virginia to make such overt confrontation as likely, but a recent
study by Richard Beeman suggests that the social and political
order of a new Piedmont county, Lunenburg, differed significantly from that of Tidewater. The leadership though drawn from
the wealthier families of the county, still had less land, fewer
slaves, less education, and a more modest style of living. Too,
although Rhys Isaac's recent study of the social and cultural
significance of the rise of the Separate Baptist movement in
Virginia, which he regards as a sharp challenge to the old Tidewater elite, does not specifically identify the evangelical upsurge
with the Piedmont, it did, in fact, cluster there in its earliest
phases, affording evidence of a popular challenge to the elite
culture and its values.[19]

What may, however, be more striking in the slightly longer run
is a strong indication that these interior regions were being drawn
in the direction of a closer resemblance to, and fuller integration
with, the coastal area of their colony. Beeman's conclusion that
the Lunenburg gentry had by the early nineteenth century further increased their average wealth and slaveholding and Isaac's
demonstration of the extent to which the enactment of religious
freedom in Virginia enabled the Baptists to shape the popular
culture of the state, coupled with the Virginia evangelicals' ultimate abandonment of opposition to slavery all point to a continued absorption of the interior into an enlarged cultural region,
although not without exercising their own influence on the resultant nineteenth-century social order.

Something of the same process occurred in the Lowcountry. It had from the first embraced the Cape Fear Region of North Carolina. Then, as James Ogelthorpe's Georgia experiment, intended to establish a colony based on small landholdings and the exclusion of slavery, broke down, coastal Georgia became an extension, too, of the Carolina Lowcountry under a separate royal government but linked to the rice producing, slave labor economy. And Rachel Klein's forthcoming study of the development of an upcountry South Carolina planter class by the first decade of the nineteenth century, traces the completion of an enlarged South Carolina cultural region. [20]

Donald Meining's *Shaping of America* labels the two enlarged regions "Greater Virginia" and "Greater South Carolina" respectively, and, except for a portion of North Carolina, assigns all of the settled area of the southern British colonies to one or the other. [21] There is still no entity we can call the colonial South, but a consolidation of five southern colonies into two dominant regions, each larger than a single colony or a state, begins a process of definition. Its advance continues into the early nineteenth century and reaches to that period when one can talk more precisely of a South, one still possessing many elements of diversity but with a regional consciousness no colonial American could have conceived.

Although there is as yet no extensive historical literature to lend detailed support to such a proposition, it seems possible to suggest, too, a way in which each of these two enlarged regions— or subregions, to continue my earlier terminology—made a further contribution to the ultimate shaping of the South, giving form to the expansionist drives that completed the definition of the extended territorial limits of the nineteenth-century South.

South Carolina, by its domination of the Indian trade with the Indians of the lower, interior South and by providing the focus of British strategic concerns in the long European imperial conflict over that region, provides a reminder that extensive penetration of the region, intercultural contact with its Indian peoples and with its small French and Spanish population, had already oc-

curred in the colonial era. The Old Southwest could plausibly be
defined as a fourth region of the colonial South, and the linkages
that would ultimately bring its acquisition and settlement had
been forged, not simply in terms of imperial conflict and expansion but by a broader process of cultural and economic exchange.[22]

Virginia by 1800 had been for a good half century the conduit
for a southward migration that would reach the lower South in
time. Settlers from Virginia, not all of whom passed through
without spending some time on Virginia lands, moved into North
Carolina, turned westward to Tennesee and Kentucky, and ultimately continued southward. The post-Revolutionary population flow became even more heavily Virginian. There were aspects, too, of its social and political organization that proved
readily adaptable to the new region—a stronger tradition of local
political institutions, an agricultural system and organization of
slavery in dispersed ownership and smaller work gangs that permitted larger planter and small farmer to share, however un-
equally, in producing a staple crop.[23]

There are other aspects of the society and culture of the southern colonies—the history of women, both black and white, the
family, the ordinary white population, the balance or tension
between the patriarchal aspirations and commercial instincts of
the planter class—where a beginning has been made in the
history of specific colonies but where a full-scale comparative
study is not yet attainable. And it will, of course, hardly be
possible ever to extend that more sharply defined, conscious
South fully into the colonial era. All of the recent argument that
colonial America generally must be perceived as having been on
the periphery of the trans-Atlantic world, comprised of a series of
isolated outposts and incompletely formed societies, argues
against regionalism anywhere in North America yet having demonstrated that degree of unifying force.

But at the same time the long-range trend was toward maturation and larger cultural regions. In the specific case of the Amer-

ican South, the significant regional groupings had been reduced
to two—if we accept Meinig's Greater Carolina and Greater Virginia. The vast interior of the British colonial South had already
begun to be absorbed into one or the other, and the Franco-
Indian zone of the lower South had experienced penetration from
Greater Carolina. Indeed both Carolina and Virginia had begun
to contribute to the expansionist thrust that would ultimately
produce the absorption of that fourth region. The process was far
from complete in 1750, or even in 1775. But much recent historical study, if only by making us look forward rather than backward, has come closer to forging the linkages that run from
colonial America to the later South.

In Search of the Family
in the Colonial South

DANIEL BLAKE SMITH

Whenever we think of southern families, what comes to mind? Honor, loyalty, pride of place, generations on the land. For Southerners, family, like community for New Englanders, has a comforting ring to it. Somehow, we believe, families have always brought a measure of certainty and purpose to life even in the most difficult times.

Perhaps they have. But until very recently it would have been hard to prove such a claim about our colonial past. For the longest time, southern family life has conjured up images rooted largely in the antebellum era—stately plantations rich in tradition and honor and paternal authority. Southern households in times past, we have been told, produced children of pride—deeply attached to the land, fiercely loyal to their families and painfully conscious of their intimate ties to an enslaved people. [1]

What, then, are we to say of *colonial* families? About the same, only cruder? Fewer slaves, less tradition. Great houses instead of stately mansions. Madeira instead of mint juleps.

I exaggerate our ignorance about these early southern families, but not by much. In the absence of a rich vein of literary sources (sermons, essays, family letters, diaries, account books, and the like) or quantitative materials (town records and birth and death records) scholars have been forced into the unpleasant task of trying to wring significance out of very little evidence. Such conditions have helped swell the ranks of New England historians.

In the past ten years or so, though—as the rising stream of New England local and family studies has overrun the banks of

21

scholarly understanding and the complex middle colonies remained as confusing as ever—a few enterprising, highly sophisticated social historians have headed South, computers and model life tables in hand, in search of a largely unexplored social and family landscape. Thanks to their pioneering efforts, it is now possible to speak with at least some confidence about the basic shape and condition of domestic life, especially in the tidewater area of early Virginia and Maryland where the surviving sources are more plentiful. Indeed, most of what I will discuss here is drawn from the rich and growing literature on the colonial Chesapeake. As we shall see, there is a great deal that we have not yet asked—let alone answered—about the inner life of these early families. But, as I also hope to show, what we now know not only breathes new life into a century and a half of family history, it also suggests that a large and intriguing distance separates these frontier families from their antebellum descendants.

I

Forming a family may seem a simple, natural thing but in the seventeenth-century South, it was a very difficult and often short-lived enterprise. Especially in the first two generations of settlement a large number of obstacles hindered, disrupted and sometimes prevented family life altogether. The very act of migration to places like the early Chesapeake placed family life in jeopardy, for it meant sundering ties to family, kin and friends in the Old World only to find early death and isolation in the New.

Unlike the New England colonies and Quaker settlements where entire families and kin groups often clustered together intact from the Old World, the South was peopled mainly by young, single, male servants brought to the New World for one purpose: to grow tobacco for their masters. If a young male servant managed to survive his seasoning in the unhealthy malarial environment of the early Chesapeake, if he could somehow

find land to rent or buy when his indenture ended, if he was
lucky enough to find an available woman to become his wife, then
he had a chance for a family.

The odds of overcoming all these problems were not good.
First, the preponderance of men in the early Chesapeake (three
or four males to every female) created long odds even for the
healthiest ex-servants with some means of financial support. On
the other hand, this unbalanced sex ratio gave women a rare and
decided advantage in the marriage market.[2]

Even more disruptive to family formation and durability were
the staggering death rates of the early South. With an endemic
malarial environment diminishing life expectancies to about the
mid 40s for adult men, many servants in the early decades of
settlement did not survive their indentures and thus never got to
compete for land or spouses. Those men who did and succeeded
in finding a bride had to contend with rather brief marriages,
perhaps only seven or eight years long, as withering death rates
did to these marriages what divorce routinely does to ours today.[3]

Harsh demographic conditions, then, severely altered family
life in the colonial South. These disordered households, distinguished by brief marriages, early parental loss, frequent re-
marriages and widespread orphanhood, could scarcely bear the
imprint of long-term parental influence. Families were mixed and
complex affairs (today we would call them "blended families"),
sometimes relying on aunts and uncles, stepparents or other kin
guardians to raise the children. This was a peculiar frontier
society, one in which widows—normally an impoverished,
powerless group in the preindustrial world—emerged sometimes
with a surprising amount of influence. They were frequently the
sole parent remaining in the household and thus possessed considerable discretion in overseeing the estate. In this chaotic,
death-ridden environment, these older women were sometimes
among the wealthiest individuals, for by outliving men and ac-
quiring their property through successive marriages, they accu-

mulated considerable economic influence. As Edmund S. Morgan has noted, this "widowarchy" created the specter of wild, young bachelors chasing after wealthy, aging women.[4]

Also contributing to this instability was the constant stream of immigrants. Unlike the family-based New England colonies, where migration was heavily concentrated in the 1630s, the Chesapeake's male-dominated immigrant stream flowed steadily throughout most of the seventeenth century, thus prolonging the chaotic, frontier stage of settlement. Combined with high death rates that did not significantly abate until after 1700, this was an immigrant society marked by impermanence. Men and women may have longed for the ties of kinship, but there were precious few relatives around to reassure them. Rituals of kinship such as weddings were often conducted not only without benefit of clergy but parents and close kin as well—for the simple reason that such people were either still in England or dead.[5]

In the absence of parental influence and kin contact, young people matured under little of the close supervision and control Englishmen clearly desired in their families. One glimpses the consequence of this relatively unstructured world in the loosened sexual restrictions of Chesapeake society: throughout much of the seventeenth century the pressure of a skewed ratio, the lack of family ties and unsettled New World conditions contributed, especially among immigrant women, to a high rate of premarital pregnancy—two or three times higher than that found among English women.[6]

Of all the peculiarities of these disrupted families, none was more conspicuous than orphanhood. Simply put, orphanhood was part of the fabric of life in the early South: perhaps one of three children lost both parents before reaching twenty-one and two of three lost one parent. And without a supporting web of kin—grandparents, uncles, aunts and family friends—it often fell upon the community itself (in the form of the Orphan's Court) to care for a large population of parentless children.[7]

Early parental death not only created an abundance of orphans, it also permitted young men to gain their independence rather early in life. Unrestrained by paternal control, surviving sons and daughters were able to make independent and early decisions about marriage and careers. In these plantation neighborhoods, the ability to marry and to establish an independent household depended largely on gaining an inheritance of land or slaves. The age, then, at which a man could marry and become self-sufficient was often closely linked to the timing of his father's death. With most fathers dying in their mid-forties, sons usually received their inheritance before they had come of age at twenty-one. Indeed, many fathers, worried that intrusive stepparents would try to "despoil the parentless," wrote wills that lowered their children's legal age to sixteen or eighteen. As a result, many young men had the opportunity and the wherewithal by their early twenties to consider marriage and assert their economic independence—several years before their counterparts in Old or New England.[8]

We should remember that all of this early independence in matters of marriage and career was thrust upon young men and women. It was not the dawning of a modern sensibility that craves autonomy and jealously guards the privacy of the conjugal family. Rather, it was a necessary adaption to a volatile, precarious world. Chesapeake parents were only too aware of the need to settle their children as quickly as possible. As Gloria Main has observed, "They sought not to bind their children to them but to enable them to stand on their own feet and to do so while still in their teens, if necessary."[9]

These were people bent on survival and little else. The very structure that planters called home suggested the evanescent quality of their lives. Family members, servants, livestock, and agricultural tools were crammed into small, dark, two- or three-room, ramshackle homes unadorned by glass windows or decoration. With only a few sticks of furniture and sometimes as many as three or four people to a bed, privacy—if it existed at all—happened *outside*, not inside the home.[10]

These abrupt, frequent changes and mixed households augured poorly for any sort of well-ordered, cohesive family. There was simply too much death, too many opportunities and too few watchful elders for the forces of authority and tradition to prevail as they so clearly did in New England and elsewhere in Anglo-America. Indeed, the seventeenth-century South was a volatile and remarkable youthful society, one that was prone to social and political unrest. "Conversation across the generations," as Peter Laslett has put it, was rare in the early South, allowing men of roughly the same age to scramble for power and wealth relatively unimpeded by a sense of tradition or a concern for the opinions of an elderly generation.[11]

Loss and change, then, came with the territory. But what did such personal disruption *mean* for these settlers in the early South? What did parents and children feel about their apparently disordered and precarious lives? Unfortunately, we do not have the direct, personal records at hand to make a persuasive answer. On the face of it, this brutal frontier would seem to be rife with trauma and anguish. And yet most historians have argued that these planters seemed to have lived lives devoid of close attachments or strong feelings for one another, even for family members. According to this view, the sheer frequency of death, along with a pervasive attitude of religious resignation cushioned the shock of so much personal loss. As William Fitzhugh solemnly declared to his mother in 1698, "Before I was ten years old . . . I look'd upon this life here as but going to an Inn, no permanent being by God's will . . . therefore am always prepared for my certain Dissolution, wch. ca'nt be perswaded to prolong by a wish."[12]

Perhaps planters assumed that their lives and the well being of their families lay not in their own hands, but in God's. Perhaps there was no time for despair or guilt. After all, children of these broken marriages found themselves launched early into independent lives of their own, just as the surviving spouse quickly found a new partner and got on with the business of everyday life. Necessity demanded it.

II

By the early decades of the eighteenth century, necessity was a much more flexible master. The third and fourth generations of planter society lived in a rather different world from these chaotic, impromptu family settings of the seventeenth century. From the surviving correspondence and personal records of the leading planters (itself indicative not only of rising literacy but also of a growing self-consciousness of personal and family matters) emerges a picture of concerned parents and dutiful children embarked on a mission of high purpose. These were men, women and children with plans and expectations for themselves and their families.

One thinks, for example, of a Richard Ambler who in 1748 laid out an elaborate education in England for his two sons while carefully reminding them of his critical role in launching them toward a life as well-bred gentlemen.

"You are now entering into Years will enable you to reflect, that many Children capable of learning, are condemn'd to the necessity of Labouring hard, for want of ability in their Parents to give them an Education. You cannot, therefore, sufficiently Adore the Divine Providence who has placed your Parents above the lower Class and thereby enabled them to be at the expence of giving you such an Education (which if not now neglected by you) will preserve you in the same Class & Rank among mankind."[13]

Among the poorer farm families, of course, paternal expectations were not so lofty, and the family itself was far less decisive in building careers or inspiring proper behavior. Yet even here families instilled meaning and shaped values among their offspring. For example, Devereux Jarratt, like most young boys of the poorer classes, found that labor not learning occupied most of his early years. Despite his family's limited ambitions for him,

Jarratt remembered domestic life in the 1740s with dignity and simple pride. "My parents neither sought nor expected any titles, honors, or great things either for themselves or children. Their highest ambition was to teach their children to read, write, and understand the fundamental rules of arithmetic. I remember also, they taught us short prayers, and made us very perfect in repeating the *Church Catechism*. They wished us all to be brought up in some honest calling, that we might earn our bread, by the sweat of our brow, as they did."[14]

The expression of such sentiments from poor and rich alike belongs to a social and familial environment quite different from the disrupted, complex households of the seventeenth century. In their own ways, Ambler and Jarratt bear witness to strong paternal influence and a more palpable sense of security among children growing up in the eighteenth century. Those coming to maturity in mid-century could expect to have more brothers and sisters, experience longer contact with their parents, find themselves surrounded by a larger supporting web of kin, and cultivate an increasingly self-conscious sense of their family lineage, what Natalie Davis calls the "family arrow in time."[15]

This family-based society of the eighteenth century was most fully realized, of course, among the wealthy planters whose large, elegant Georgian homes advertised their genteel refinement and family pride. Among the planter gentry the evidence for this stable, patriarchal family system was everywhere: in the more compact, densely settled neighborhoods which promoted increasing kin contact—including cousin marriage; in the larger houses that emphasized the differential use of domestic space, especially segregating the public parlor from private bedrooms; in the deliberate family strategy of fathers who successfully bequeathed land and slaves to protect the economic futures of their children; and in the kin-oriented naming patterns in which parents increasingly named their offspring in honor of the family line.[16]

The emerging patriarchy clearly benefitted sons more than

daughters. While young planters' sons rambled about the plantation, immersing themselves in the public world of the court-
house, the local store and the tavern, daughters quietly inhabited
the much more private world of the home. Growing up female in
planter families meant learning to become the compliant, agreeable helpmate for a husband. Among the well to do, a daughter's
education might extend beyond basic literacy to include dancing
and drawing and music, but even here (for girls such as Thomas
Jefferson's daughter, Martha) the goal was to cultivate accomplished, lady-like skills that would complement, not compete
with, those possessed by men.[17]

In 1770 Mary Ambler of Virginia transcribed the following
portion of a "Sermon to a Young Woman" for her daughter, who
she hoped would read and "observe it well all her Life." It could
have been the credo for most well-to-do women in colonial America: "If to Your natural softness You join that christian meekness
. . . both together will not fail, with the assistance of proper
reflection and friendly advice, to accomplish you in the best &
truest breeding. You will not be in danger of putting your-selves
forward in company, of contradicting bluntly, of asserting
positively, of debating obstinately, of affecting a superiority to any
present, of engrossing the discourse, of listening to yourselves
with apparent satisfaction, of neglecting what is advanced by
others, or of interrupting them without necessity."[18]

This was a society that launched sons and polished daughters.
In the colonial South a woman's unique role lay in her lifelong
commitment to pleasing the men around her and to ensuring a
harmonious, stable family.

It is always easier, of course, to describe change than to explain
it. The emergence of this stable, patriarchal family system in the
early eighteenth century seemed to derive from several con-
verging economic and demographic trends: lengthening life
spans, the development of a native-born society, and the large-
scale introduction of slave labor.

The improved disease environment of the eighteenth century

South did not make for the near-modern life expectancies found in colonial New England, but the differences were narrowing. Where settlers had commonly died in their mid-forties during the seventeenth century, by the early 1700s planters could expect to live well into their fifties. With this greater longevity came more enduring ties between spouses and between parents and children. Watchful parents could now successfully transmit values as well as property to the rising generation. Perhaps for the first time, parents could shape their children in their own images.[19]

Yet another boon to family and kinship was the emergence of a native-born society. By the 1690s most areas in the Chesapeake achieved what demographers call "generational replacement," as sex ratios began to even out and native-born adults for the first time surpassed the number of immigrants. No longer dependent on a steady flow of new settlers to populate the region, Chesapeake society began to pass out of the frontier era into a much more stable, settled society. Intricate kin networks developed in plantation neighborhoods, providing for the first time a multi-generational world of relatives who could help socialize children and provide aid and comfort in times of stress.[20]

Finally, the growing reliance on slaves allowed middling and well-to-do planters a more leisured domestic existence. Indeed, the acquisition of slaves in planter households gradually eliminated much of women's economic value on the plantation, confining them more and more to the home where they were urged to fulfill their child-bearing and child-rearing obligations. As noted before, women may actually have possessed more economic authority in the seventeenth century when their relative scarcity made them especially attractive in the marriage and labor markets. By the early decades of the eighteenth century, however, a balanced sex ratio and the increasing reliance on slave labor offered southern women little more than the opportunity to become agreeable companions for their husbands and useful mothers to their children.[21]

In all likelihood, the presence of servants and house slaves to help in child-rearing and discipline in the household made it easier for parents to be indulgent and affectionate toward their children. Planters' wives, freed of most of the heavy field work and aided in the kitchen and garden by house slaves, focused their attention on motherhood. Children now took on an increasingly modern role in their parents eyes—that of affectionate, special people—and became the emotional focus of the family.

III

Unquestionably, families organized themselves and behaved in different ways as the frontier period gave way to more settled conditions in the eighteenth century. But what do these changes in the family really tell us about attitudes and values or about the family's relation to the world beyond the household—in society and politics?

Historians have long recognized the pivotal role of familial politics in the South, especially in the eighteenth century. And the recent wave of work on the social history of the colonial Chesapeake has helped explain why family dynasties first appeared in the eighteenth century. In the disease-ridden seventeenth century, death often abruptly ended political careers. But with the emergence of a native-born population and longer life spans after 1700, family dynasties could finally develop as access to high office depended increasingly on one's family name and connections. The slaveholding planter gentry, bound together by marriage and class interests, created a political cousinry that dominated political life from the county courts to the House of Burgesses.[22]

This increasingly family and kin-based society also reflected sharpened class consciousness in the eighteenth century. According to Rhys Isaac, the great landed families of the mid-eighteenth century deliberately set themselves off in elegant, refined great houses that served as "sacrosanct settings for hospitality" and the open display of the greatness of the "family and the magnanimity of its head." Isaac claims that families such as the Byrds, Carters and Lees—with their "symmetrically-retained dependencies and self-sufficient rural communities"—conceived of their estates as rural retreats from a world of the unworthy. Such monuments to the egos and prestige of the gentry, he argues, created an "aura of the great house," and constituted a rich, symbolic means for gentry families to enhance their own "individual separateness," while cultivating a distinctive, class-conscious lifestyle superior to the common folk.[23]

It probably comes as no surprise that great landed families of the period built lavish homes as physical evidence of their genteel social standing. But what, exactly, went on inside their elegant great houses? In trying to probe the social values and emotions of planter families, historians have offered speculation but little else. Seizing upon the most conspicuous distinction in southern families—the presence of slaves in and out of the great house—some historians have argued that the "command experience" encouraged in planters' sons a powerful streak of independence, self-confidence and proud assertiveness. According to this view, slaveholding in gentry families nurtured personal mastery that by 1776 helped turn proud planters into staunch patriots.[24]

If planters and their offspring displayed themselves as competitive, self-confident, liberty-loving individuals, they did so with cool detachment around the house. According to Jan Lewis, pre-Revolutionary Virginia families had only one obsession in life: the establishment of "domestic tranquility." The savagery of the frontier, she claims, still lay uncomfortably close at hand—even among the refined gentry class—and so they busily pursued graceful ways inside their Georgian homes, so as to blot out all the brutality and incivility that surrounded them. In doing so, she argues, planter families became peaceable kingdoms characterized by self-restraint, stifled emotions and rare intimacy. From the formal, calculated grandiloquence of courtship to the calm resignation in times of death, *la vie intime* among the planter class suggested a rather cold, astringent atmosphere.[25]

Lewis certainly exaggerates the sense of restraint and moderation in planter households—ignoring, for example, the indulgent affection eighteenth-century parents lavished on their children, as well as the private passions between husbands and wives. Nonetheless, she rightly points to an intriguing tension among families in the early eighteenth century: the search for peace and harmony amid discord and passion.

Much of this tension was played out in open, expansive family settings rather than the private, intimate home life that became increasingly common in the late eighteenth century. An extreme example of the inclusive, public nature of these planter patriarchies is William Byrd's domestic life at Westover. As a man who gloried in playing the patriarch to a large number of dependents—white and black, free and slave—Byrd spent much of his time away from home out in the fields supervising slaves and overseers or engaging in countless rounds of visitation, often ignoring his wife and children. For Byrd, family was not the private, intimate circle of close kin gathered in affection around hearth and home; rather, he understood family life in a looser, much more diffuse fashion, as an essentially public phenomenon, a kind of constant sociability and companionship with likeminded people with whom he shared important work and leisure moments in the plantation community.[26]

But Byrd's peaceful patriarchy frequently gave way to conflict and chaos. His diary suggests a family life that was full of violent quarreling with his wife and servants, frequent whippings of black and white servants and aggressive sexual conduct aimed at control rather than love. The peaceful, well-ordered family may have been the ideal, but it was an ideal that was dashed by the difficult realities of everyday life.[27]

Which is to say that when we look back on the first century and a half of southern family and society we find that most men and women grew up in households marked as much by disruption as stability, by discord as well as harmony, by stark simplicity alongside elegant refinement. For most men, women and children of the early South, families were not safe havens or warm and comforting social units set safely apart from a harsh outside world; their families were inescapably tied to that precarious world, a world where illness and death disrupted marriages and orphaned children, and where for over two generations only the hardiest sons and daughters grew to maturity—and often without the shaping influence of those who brought them into the world.

And in the life of those few gentry families of the eighteenth century in which leisure and refinement conferred a measure of purpose and control, wild, unsettled forces could spring up all around. As Bernard Bailyn has recently observed, American settlers, even in the more stable golden age, found themselves caught between a "state of self-conscious gentility" and "the violence and extravagance and disorder of life in a marchland." Bailyn's provocative image of Thomas Jefferson, enlightened slaveholder, "looking out from Queen Anne rooms of spare elegance into wild, uncultivated land," suggests, among other things, that the family may well have been an especially important means for staving off the still untamed forces at work.[28]

What was Jefferson thinking, Bailyn wonders? I don't know. But the question is a powerful and challenging one, for it forces us to look beyond structure, behavior and symbol—life expectancy, slaveholding, housing styles—and to inquire as well into matters of the heart. The evidence for such an inquiry is scarce indeed, but without such insight what do we really know about these planters and their families?

Despite all the sophisticated research of the past ten to fifteen years, there is a great deal that we do not know and, worse yet, I fear that the unknown may well be essential for truly understanding these colonial families. What we do not know, of course, has as much to do with severe source limitations as it does with limited historical imagination. Social historians, perhaps more than most, labor at the mercy of their sources. And the sources in early southern family life are simply—and perhaps significantly—

silent about so much. Assessing the unsaid—the intimacies and private hopes and fears—is a critical if daunting task.

A host of intriguing but as yet unanswerable questions come to mind about these early southern families. What were the emotional implications of so much disease and death in planter households? How did these apparently chaotic, ever-shifting family settings in the seventeenth century affect the rearing of children or the perception of parenthood? In trying to recover the emotional texture of these precarious, evanescent family arrangements perhaps we have erred in looking so hard for rare glimpses into the private moments inside the household. Could it be, especially in the early South, that the central, shaping forces of these men and women lay not in their crowded, sparsely-furnished homes but *outside* in the tobacco fields, courthouses and taverns? Perhaps the history of *la vie intime* cannot be told in these early years for the simple reason that there was so little of it.

With the emergence of a stable, family-based society in the eighteenth century we have at hand considerably more direct, personal evidence, but the unknowns loom just as large. Except for a few unusual planters like Landon Carter and William Byrd, we have no sense of the passion and sexual values that shaped perceptions about gender, family and personal identity. The same can be said for religious experience. At present, scholars assume on the basis of a general silence in the documents that religious values counted for little in planter households. But in a largely oral culture one wonders how much deeply-felt piety never found written expression. Finally, and perhaps most conspicuous, is our ignorance about masters and slaves inside the great house. Did the presence of house slaves significantly alter the tenor of family relations? To date, our best insight comes from Jefferson who gave voice to parental fears of exposing children to the brutalizing and ruthless business of commanding slaves: "The parent storms, the child looks on, catches the lineaments of wrath, puts on the same airs in the circle of smaller slaves, gives a loose to his worst passions, and thus nursed, educated, and daily exercised in tyranny, cannot but be stamped by it with odious peculiarities."[29]

Does Jefferson's psychological insight reveal slavery's most intimate and powerful consequence—at least among whites? If so, we should expect planter families to be more highly charged than they appear to be in the surviving correspondence and diaries. As it stands, the silence of planters on the subject of slaves suggests that they were regarded more as fixed objects on the master's family landscape—almost like pieces of furniture—than as significant, potentially volatile human actors in the family drama. The problem of assessing the unsaid is perhaps greatest here—in confronting the daily experience and impact of slaves in planter households. The silence of the documents on the master-slave relationship is overwhelming and remains one of the biggest disappointments for historians of the family in the colonial South.

Until we begin to develop the means to address such fundamental aspects of domestic existence in the early South, we can not effectively explore larger interpretive themes about the family in southern society. It is a long way from these children of chaos of the seventeenth century to the children of pride two centuries later. Our task, then, is not only to understand the roots and changing meaning of patriarchalism or paternalism or any other "ism," it is first to recover the life of the family. In doing so, we may discover that all our theorizing is but a convenient label blindly affixed to a complex, dimly-understood phenomenon. Which is to say that making generalizations about family life in the past is always a dangerous and difficult endeavor. To think broadly widens our vision of aggregate patterns and general directions, but it discloses nothing of the individual experiences—all the private hopes and fears—which, truth to tell, make families what they are.

Three Planters and Their Slaves: Perspectives on Slavery in Virginia, South Carolina, and Jamaica, 1750-1790

PHILIP MORGAN

Despite its dethronement in the realm of political theory, patriarchalism was a vibrant social ethos in eighteenth-century British America, particularly in plantation America. The patriarchal outlook suffused the thought of the age, running the gamut from the unstated prejudices of the silent masses to the well-ordered and self-conscious theories of a thinker like Jonathan Boucher.[1] It is undeniable that contractual reciprocity rather than rigid authoritarianism had begun to characterize eighteenth-century family relations, but the sway of the father was still powerful. Family life only gradually became more egalitarian, domesticated, and sentimental.[2] Moreover, even while the smaller family unit was becoming less patriarchal, the larger families of the more substantial planters were growing ever larger and more consequential. With the number of dependents growing apace, patriarchal doctrines assumed even more resonance. In short, a profound respect for rank, hierarchy, and status infused the very marrow of the early modern Anglo-American world, and at its core lay the authority of the father-figure in his own household.

In fact, manuals of household government were dominated by patriarchal doctrines. They spoke of servants as subservient members of the family, living under the authority of the *paterfamilias*. Gentlemen were cautioned not to let their care stop at their own children; "let it reach to your menial servants," they

37

were instructed, for "though you are their master, you are also
their father." Servants, on the other hand, heard that they were
"only concerned in *one* matter, to do the work that lies before
them, whilst others have a *world* of things to look on, and look
after."[3] This advice about servants could extend to slaves. Not for
nothing had slaves been termed *famuli* in the ancient world. They
were the original *familia*, a group of *famuli* living under the same
roof, from whence the modern term derives. Eighteenth-century
Anglo-American masters were simply party to this tradition when
they referred to their slaves as their "people," their "folks," or as
part of their "family."[4]

Not that Anglo-American masters confused slaves with servants, of course. The very fact that a slave was a lifetime chattel
necessarily placed him more fully at the absolute disposal of his
master—a status beyond the wildest dreams of a master of servants. Whereas English masters attempted to counteract the
profound instability of their servant class, colonial masters had
essentially created a dependent class forbidden to move.
Whereas some English masters sought registration laws and pass-
ports for their servants, colonial masters could point to skin color
as a far more effective insignia of dependency. Whereas English
masters petitioned for stiffer punishments for intractable servants, colonial masters could punish almost at will within the
confines of their own plantations. And, whereas English masters
provided wages, decent shelter, adequate food, and perhaps fine
livery for their servants, colonial masters offered minimal subsistence to their slaves. In theory, and to a large extent in practice,
colonial masters exercised almost unlimited dominion over their
charges.[5]

Ironically, precisely because a slave entered into no contractual
relationship with his master but was instead subject to direct
personal domination, the familial mode seemed all the more
appropriate to his situation. Consider that slaves were almost
uniformly known by familial, not formal, names—Jack for John,
Matt for Mathew, Sukey for Susanna, and so on—not to mention

the absence of surnames.[6] The slave was not simply a factor of production with whom the employer maintained a limited relationship—a condition that was becoming familiar to some laborers in eighteenth-century Anglo-America—he was part of the master's household. True, slaves were chattel and masters could and did think of them in the language of property. True, Anglo-American masters were extremely profit-conscious, operated in a market economy, and therefore employed the language of commercial capitalism. But neither discourse nor consideration overrode, though both certainly intruded upon, the masters' sense of slaves as dependents. Being part of a household served to cushion slaves from the full force of free market commercialism. Harsh profit-and-loss purgatives had not yet voided this world of its traditional notions of duty, mutuality, and patriarchal care. This is not to engage in sentimentality or idealization for, as we shall see, the persistence of these notions was not always to the slaves' advantage. It is, however, to confront the reality of the eighteenth-century world, as masters conceived it.[7]

The pervasiveness of patriarchal attitudes in eighteenth-century British America does not mean that the master-slave relationship should be viewed statically or homogeneously. Slavery, like any other social institution, cannot be divorced from time and place. Indeed, slavery was almost infinitely variegated over time, across space, and within social groups. Since these three themes—the temporal, spatial, and social dimensions of slavery—are interwoven throughout the body of this essay, a word or two is in order about the underlying arguments.

First, if patriarchalism is the key to understanding master-slave relations in the eighteenth century, as I believe it is, it is nevertheless true that patriarchal attitudes were in the throes of being reformulated in the latter half of the century. The shift, to use shorthand, from patriarchalism to paternalism can be seen in embryo toward the close of the century. This distinction between patriarchalism and paternalism may seem a fine one, but at least three key differences separate the two. First, patriarchalism was a more austere code than paternalism. Patriarchal masters stressed order, authority, unswerving obedience, and were quick to resort to violence when their authority was questioned. Paternal masters were not exactly anti-authoritarian or non-violent, but were more inclined to stress their solicitude, their generous treatment of their dependents. Second, if patriarchalism was a more severe code than paternalism, it was also less constricting. Eighteenth-century slaves undoubtedly suffered worse material conditions than their nineteenth-century counterparts, but patriarchs rarely spoke in cloying and claustrophobic terms of their kindness or their Christian trusteeship toward their slaves. Paternal masters, on the other hand, expected gratitude, even love from their slaves; they were keenly interested in their slaves' religious welfare; their outlook was far more sentimental. Third, patriarchs never underestimated their slaves' capacity to rebel; unlike paternalists, they rarely boasted of the submissiveness or docility of their slaves. Paternalists created the fiction of the contented and happy slave. This stark demarcation between two outlooks, two ideologies—one confined to the eighteenth, the other to the nineteenth, century—is much too neat. These are models, ideal types; in reality, the situation was far more complex and confused. This was particularly true late in the century when the shift from one to the other was underway, though it was not to be completed until well into the nineteenth century.[8]

Just as master-slave relations changed over time, so they varied across space—this is the second leitmotif. Some regions encouraged a more personal relationship between master and slave; others were characterized by far more distanced contact. These differences arose from a large number of forces, most of which can only be hinted at in the brief space allotted here. Perhaps most important, however, was a region's staple crop, which influenced everything from the size of plantations to the proportion of slaves in the total population. Almost as important were a region's mix of Africans and creoles, its settlement patterns, its climate, as well as the personal temperament of individual masters. Consequently, even within the same Anglo-American culture, the relations of masters and slaves could vary enormously from one society to another.

Just as masters can be grouped into various types, so can slaves—this is the third theme. Various groups and statuses existed within the body of people so easily homogenized as slaves. There were foremen, house servants, artisans, the elderly, children, just to mention a few of the more obvious classifications. A master's relationship with his slaves might vary markedly depending on which group or representative of a group he encountered. In fact, it is suggested in this essay that masters in very different societies had rather similar relationships with certain types of slaves. Contrary to the general stress on changes over time and place, some master-slave relationships seem almost impervious to such variations.

Perhaps the best way to explore these themes, and to discover the individuality of ordinary people and the particularity of local communities, is to pursue a number of case studies. To this end, I propose a microscopic investigation, focusing on three central figures: Landon Carter (1710-1778), Henry Laurens (1724-1792), and Thomas Thistlewood (1721-1786). Through the lens of their individual lives, we can catch glimpses of three groups of slaves, three sets of master-slave interactions, three slave systems in action. In other words, I hope to probe in brief compass the range of possibilities, the variations, and the commonalities of British American slavery in the second half of the eighteenth century.

Carter, Laurens, and Thistlewood shared a number of characteristics. They all lived to about the same age—their mid-sixties. Each one of them spent a formative part of his life in England. Their mature years spanned roughly the same period of time, i.e., the third quarter of the eighteenth century. During these twenty-five years or more, each resided in one of three major plantation societies of Anglo-America: Virginia, South Carolina, and Jamaica. They each spent a considerable part of their lives managing plantations. Above all, this meant managing labor,

largely in the persons of slaves. The lives of these three white
planters were, therefore, inextricably intertwined with, indelibly
imprinted by, their black slaves. Through the prism of three lives,
we can see refracted the experiences of three groups of black
slaves.

It would be futile, of course, to deny the differences between
our three dramatis personae and the ways they make themselves
known to us. Carter and Laurens established major fortunes and
played notable roles on the political stage; Thistlewood eventually
established himself as a gentleman, a member of his parish
vestry, and a justice of the peace, but his stage was local, not
national. Carter and Thistlewood were farmers; Laurens was first
and foremost a merchant, who came to agriculture late in life.
Carter and Thistlewood lived in the countryside; Laurens lived
for the most part in town, only retiring to a plantation at the very
end of his life. Carter and Laurens were creoles; Thistlewood an
immigrant. We also learn of the three in rather different ways:
Carter via an extremely personal diary into which he poured his
frustrations; Laurens largely through the medium of routine business and occasional personal correspondence; Thistlewood by
means of a matter-of-fact daily journal.

At once alike, since they were planters in the same Anglo-
phone world, and yet significantly different, since they inhabited
radically different environments, these three masters and their
slaves can provide intelligent commentaries upon one another.
Each looks different in light of the other; and our understanding
of each is enlarged by knowledge of the other.

I

Landon Carter seems to have begun keeping a diary around the
middle of the century. By then, he possessed an immense estate,
with its hub located in Richmond County in the Northern Neck
region of Virginia. Like all large Chesapeake planters, Carter ran
an extraordinarily dispersed farming operation. At its center lay
Sabine Hall, and within striking distance various satellite com-

munities—the home, Fork, and Mangorike quarters—but, beyond that, there were at least another eight quarters stretching
out into other parts of the Northern Neck, the York peninsula,
and the northern Piedmont. In 1779, when Carter's estate was
inventoried, he possessed 401 slaves scattered through nine separate counties.[9]

Throughout the course of his known diary-keeping (effectively
just over twenty years), Carter referred to about 180 slaves by
name: 165 belonged to him (though, in the case of 9, a common
name and lack of other distinguishing information make it unclear
whether he is speaking of the same slave or two separate individuals), 13 belonged to neighboring masters, and 3 might not have
been slaves at all.[10] Most of these 180 were mentioned only once
or twice (most commonly for ill health); rarely did he refer to a
slave from, say, York or Northumberland counties, the locations of
some of his larger quarters; rather, the slaves about whom he
spoke most often held some form of privileged position, either as
house servant, artisan, carter, or foreman, upon the home estate.
Of these, about 10 slaves formed an inner core, with whom
Carter had regular and intense encounters.[11] To see patriarchalism in action, we might investigate three types of master-
slave encounters.

Like many masters, Carter had a particularly intense relationship with one slave, a personal body servant. In Carter's case,
this man was named Nassau. Nassau was Carter's constant companion, his alter ego, almost part of his very identity. Nassau
inspected crops, counted and branded livestock, administered
the occasional whipping, but, primarily, acted as the plantation's
chief medical aide both to slaves and to lower-class whites. Carter
was even willing to use his assistant's services himself, since
"Nassau [was] the best bleeder about."[12] Carter and Nassau
shared a great deal. The master came to know that his slave
fervently disliked snakes; the two of them discussed and often
disagreed on medical diagnoses; one Sunday found the two of
them walking about the home fields exchanging observations on

the quality of the tobacco; and Carter valued his assistant's judgment, recording proudly that "Dr Nassau says he has seen much tobacco, and never saw any stand better."[13]

If Nassau's responsibilities were great, so were his frailties. He was, in fact, a chronic alcoholic. Living in such proximity to a demanding master undoubtedly took its toll. On one occasion, Carter remarked that Nassau had "not been sensibly sober one evening since this day fortnight." On another, Carter described Nassau crawling about the room at night, not knowing "a chamber pot from a bottle of water."[14] The master's attempts to deal with this problem reveal the intimacy of their relationship. Carter did not just threaten Nassau, he "begged him, Prayed him and told him the consequences if he neglected the care to one of the sick people." Their conversations even led Carter to examine his own conduct. "I confess I have faults myself to be forgiven," Carter acknowledged, "but to every day and hour committing them, and to seek the modes of committing them [i.e., searching out liquor] admits of no Plea of frailty." And yet Nassau continued to drink "in spight" of Carter, even as the master dimly understood, "in order to spight [him]."[15]

The long-running battle between the stern and sober patriarch and his valued but frequently drunken personal servant, tortuous as it must have been to both parties, assumes almost farcical dimensions as it unfolds to us through the master's diary. In 1768 Nassau's drunkenness became public knowledge when Carter unburdened himself in the pages of the *Virginia Gazette* about a prospective vacancy in his household:

> My man Nassau who I have with much care bred up to be of great service amongst my sick people, having fallen into a most abandoned state of drunkenness, and indeed injured his constitution by it, is become now rather a prejudice to me, as he cannot be trusted in the business he has been long practiced in. As I intend to indulge his appetite, which cannot be cured of by any persuasion, I will, as soon as I can, send him to some of the islands where no doubt he may get his liquor with less pains than he seems to take.[16]

Carter, not for the last time, relented, and Nassau continued in his employ. But the bouts of drunkenness persisted—as did the master's vacillations. In the fall of 1770, Carter engaged in another of his many self-deceptions. "I have been learning to do without [Nassau]," he noted, "though it has been but very badly yet I can bear it and will." Three years later, he vowed never to pass over another instance of Nassau's insobriety.[17]

In 1775 the most dramatic scene occurred. Nassau, found "dead drunk," was brought home, whereupon the sixty-five-year-old patriarch in sheer frustration,

> offered to give him a box on the ear and he fairly forced himself against me. However I tumbled him into the Sellar and there had him tied Neck and heels all night and this morning had him stripped and tied up to a limb and, with a Number of switches Presented to his eyes and a fellow with an uplifted arm, he encreased his crying Petitions to be forgiven but this once, and desired the man to bear witness that he called on God to record his solemn Vow that he never more would touch liquor. I expostulated with him on his and his father's blasphemy of denying the wholy word of God in bolding asserting that there was neither a hell nor a devil, and asked him if he did not dread to hear how he had set the word of God at nought who promised everlasting happiness to those who loved him and obeyed his words and eternal torments who set his goodness at nought and dispised his holy word. After all I forgave this creature out of humanity, religion, and every virtuous duty with hopes though I hardly dare mention it that I shall by it save one soul more Alive.[18]

Almost exchanging blows one minute, appealing to God in forgiveness the next—such could be the demands of an intense master–personal servant relationship.

No reformation was wrought, of course. Nassau continued to drink and Carter, though bitter at his servant's "forfeit[ing] his solemn Promise before heaven," could still not bear to part with him. In the fall of 1775, Carter's ambivalent feelings toward Nassau were summed up in one and the same sentence: "If he

goes, I shall be rid of a Villain, though a most capable servant." A
year and a half later, Carter "for the last time excused [Nassau] on
a most [sol]emn Promise never more to drink." A couple of weeks
later, Nassau tried to disguise the alcohol on his breath by chew-
ing "new tobacco." He was not successful, but he hardly need
have bothered. A few months before Carter's death in 1778, we
find him still lamenting that Nassau "is proof against his oaths
never to drink." Only death would intervene to part Carter and
Nassau.[19]

A second common type of encounter was between master and
skilled slave, whether woodworker, plowman, or the like. This
relationship was almost always fraught with ambivalence. On the
one hand, the slave with a skill inevitably earned a measure of
respect from his master. Take Manuel, for instance, whom Carter
considered to be "the best plowman and mower [he] ever saw."
Manuel often told his master just when he would finish plowing a
field, an indication of how much he set his own pace. He was an
adept sower of seed. On one occasion, Carter praised Manuel for
"prudently" leaving off sowing rye until it could be hoed into the
ground. Once when Carter was watching Manuel plowing corn
rows, the master could not but marvel at the huge clods produced
by his deep plowing. "[R]eally it is good work," exclaimed an
admiring master. Carter also entrusted Manuel with important
errands, as in fetching brandy and molasses from fellow planters
or in taking live animals to them.[20]

On the other hand, a skilled slave generally found many opportunities to exploit his privileged position. In Manuel's case, his
"villainy" extended from carelessness to outright flouting of his
master's authority. If he was not attempting to kill off Carter's
oxen and horses by miring them in mud, he was breaking his
carts and going slow at his work.[21] Manuel seems to have lost all
respect for planter authority, not just because Carter never
fulfilled his threats to sell him, but because he managed to evade
the hangman's noose on no fewer than three occasions. On the
first, Carter prosecuted Manuel for breaking and entering his

own storehouse. Found guilty, marched up to the gallows, the halter placed around his neck, Manuel barely escaped with his life when the Governor's pardon was announced. On a subsequent occasion, the law itself allowed Manuel to slip through its grasp. Although stolen goods were found in Manuel's possession, their provenance could not be determined, and the case was dismissed. After a third trial for felony and his second death sentence, Carter invested £16 to secure a second reprieve. He justified this act of mercy on the grounds that he was shorthanded, "it being the smallpox time." After all this, it should hardly surprise us that Manuel took up Lord Dunmore's invitation to seek freedom with the British.[22]

A third common type of encounter was that between a master and his elderly slaves. Eighteenth-century Anglo-America was a young man's world. Elderly people were a rarity, and perhaps elicited a measure of respect as a result. This applied even to slaves. Landon Carter's Jack Lubbar is a good case in point. Their two lives had intertwined as early as the 1730s when Carter had found Jack "too old a man to keep as a foreman." Gradually, Carter had lightened his old slave's workload, until, in the master's characteristically self-regarding words, Jack lived "quite retired only under my constant kindness." But Jack continued to inspire his master's admiration by being as active as ever:

> he . . . became a vast progger in Catching fish, Beavers, otters, Muskrats, and Minxes with his traps, a Constant church man in all good days and as erect and fast a Walker as almost any man in the Parish. In this manner has the good old man continued with as well a stored garden and patches of pease and belly timber, as it is called, and has spent the latter part of his time till about a fortnight ago he hurt his shin.

On the whole, Jack seems to have been on good terms with younger slaves. As an "overlooker" at the Fork quarter he managed to inspire his charges to produce unusually large crops. On one occasion, Carter even contrasted his own unhappy experience as a father to his slave's, for Jack had been "blessed with his children's company." However, this did not apparently extend to his grandchildren or great-grandchildren. Jack had remained at Fork quarter until "his age almost deprived him of eyesight which made him desire to be removed because those under him, mostly his great grandchildren, by the baseness of their Parents abused him much."[23]

Masters developed special relationships with those few slaves with whom they shared so much of their adult lives. For one thing, elderly slaves proved valuable repositories of information. Landon Carter listened to the "old Stagers" in his field gangs, because their knowledge of agricultural matters was often superior to that of their white overseers. Not that he always trusted them. Once, when "talking to my old people" about their worming and topping of a particular tobacco patch, Carter doubted that all was as well as he was told. When Carter voiced his suspicions, old Sukey answered in no uncertain terms that she "knew the ground" and "would answer" for a good crop come September. The following day, Carter's suspicious mind would not rest, and he again accused his slaves of deception. Sukey's patience ran out, and the following exchange took place:

> Sukey told me . . . she would be hanged if any planter seeing that ground would not say the tobacco stood tollerably well. I told her it was too small. She replied she knew the ground, knew how it was dunged, and would be hanged if it did not turn out good Tobacco.

Carter seems to have been reassured and turned to wondering whether the soil itself was not too stiff.[24]

These three examples give the flavor of Carter's style of interaction with his slaves—and a particular version of the patriarchal disposition. The style was severe, for, while the master felt under many obligations to his charges, he also had the right, nay the responsibility, to exact swift retribution should they not obey. Carter assumed an adjudicatory, magisterial air, administering his own form of household justice. He seemed to be always threatening, cajoling, and punishing his slaves for actual or suspected transgressions. Transgressions there certainly were. The act of running away was mentioned fifty-two times in Carter's diary over a twenty-three-year period. Most of the runaways were short-term absentees, to be sure, and at least fourteen ran away under the special circumstances of the Revolutionary war; nevertheless, a fifth of all the slaves mentioned by Carter ran away at least once, at least four were outlawed and liable to be shot on sight, while a few like Johnny "by lying out for months contracted ganglins in his leggs" or George who "was for ten years a noted runaway, always in the woods and mostly naked," made it their career.[25] Punishments were also common. In the year 1770 alone—much the fullest of any in the diary—over twenty separate whippings of about thirty slaves were reported. Runaway Guy, for instance, had his correction "in sight of the people."[26]

Severity also characterized work discipline on Carter's quarters. Carter carefully monitored the labor of his slaves. His diversified farming regime meant that slaves were kept busy all year at a variety of tasks. On occasion, their work extended into the night. Hanging tobacco in the fall and stemming it in winter saw slaves working well past midnight.[27] The master of Sabine Hall even engaged in primitive time and motion studies. One June day in 1770 saw Carter watch his gangs in three two-hour stretches in order to gauge their progress in turning tobacco hills. He often mentioned the hour at which slaves began or ended a certain task as he attempted to ascertain labor input. He had fairly well defined daily expectations for any given task.[28] He mobilized all his able-bodied laborers, putting to work not just men, but women and children above the age of ten. Some gangs consisted solely of women; twelve-year-old Ambrose worked in the field; one gang of twenty-three hands included eight boys and girls.[29] Carter took his role as taskmaster seriously.

And yet Carter's efforts to regiment his work force were far from successful. For one thing, his slaves were often sick or feigned sickness, so that much labor was lost. At one point, Carter noted grimly that slaves seemed particularly prone to illness on Monday mornings, never Sundays when they "don't care to be confined by physick." On another occasion, he merely recorded, "[m]any hands pretend to be sick," though "persuaded all but two to go out."[30] For another, the mode of labor employed in the Chesapeake, namely ganging, had many inherent deficiencies. It required that a "principal hand" set the pace. Should that slave fall sick or work slowly, the whole gang moved at reduced speed. Carter was constantly railing at these "conductor[s] of . . . idleness."[31] Both these examples raise a common stumbling-block to Carter's aspirations: his workers. His diary is a litany of complaints about the carelessness, neglectfulness, sheer "lazyness," to adopt his terminology, of his laborers. They conspired to slow the work-pace at every turn.[32] Finally, however, Carter himself was not quite the hard-driving employer he liked to appear. He continued to reward certain slaves, even when he recognized that his actions produced no increase, if anything a decline, in diligence. Occasionally, he allowed a holiday on Saturday.[33] He "indulged" his slaves on particularly inclement days. "I can't make my people work or do any thing," he noted one July day, "indeed the 3 past days so hot I could not desire."[34] The supposed harsh driver of men did not always live up to his billing.

There was, in other words, a less severe side to the patriarchal disposition. Indeed, at its most elevated, the patriarchal ethos aimed to be an uplifting creed. The master offered to protect, guard, and care for his charges, thereby fulfilling a powerful and ancient image of master as provider. Indeed, offering "protection" was itself a survival of feudal terminology that recalled the ancient origins of the concept of family. After lightning struck Sabine Hall in 1773, Carter re-created, with some embellishment no doubt, the "dismal" scene for his imaginary readers. At the center of the ensuing bedlam stood a calm, undaunted patriarch, surrounded by a mother calling for her babes, many grand-children "with every sorrowful countenance," and "Poor slaves crowding round and following their master, as if *protection* only came from him." Carter drew his own moral: "God was merciful, and I hope it will not be misplaced on anyone who saw this sight at least."[35] God looked kindly on patriarchs.

For Carter, no other aspect of his slaves' lives concerned him more than their health. His interest extended far beyond the impersonal prescription of drugs or the careful recounting of sums outlaid on his chattels' welfare. Of course, the safeguarding of a valuable asset was uppermost in his mind. Nor were his actions always benevolent. Carter used harsh drugs on his slaves that he would not countenance for his own children.[36] At the same time, he involved himself too personally and with too much care for us to dismiss his behavior as no more than a calculating regard for pieces of property. To "feel and examine" a slave, as he did with his house servant Joe, was not unusual. To see him closely monitoring symptoms and dispensing medicines, as he did on numerous occasions, is to know that much of his self-image was bound up in these tasks. A hint of this self-image importance is revealed when he, to "humour other people" [perhaps slaves?], called in two doctors to treat a slave for a particularly intractable case of nosebleeding. Carter had no great expectations about the doctors' expertise, but acceded to the request because "it is the duty of a Master."[37]

As an example, consider Carter's interest in the health of his old house servant, Mulatto Betty, who was often sick. During Betty's bouts of illness, Carter would often visit her at least twice a day; once put his own chariot at her disposal so that she could take the air when too weak to ride; questioned the doctor's prescriptions on the grounds that this so-called professional did not understand the temperament of his patient who was "a nice Lady and only wanted to be made much of"; and, finally, turned angry when his ungrateful patient would not follow his directions to the letter. At that point, Carter "sent her word to get well how she could," declared he would not "Practice on her," and adopted a self-righteous stance that "I would save her; but she will not let me."[38]

This self-righteousness assumed even greater proportions

when Carter reflected "on his own conduct" to a group of nine runaways who answered Lord Dunmore's proclamation in 1776. Predictably, Carter could find no fault with himself; rather, he believed his avoidance of any "kind of Severity" should only "have taught them gratitude." In four of the nine runaways, Carter singled out his healing powers as cause enough for gratitude. Thus, Carter recalled that his own "care constantly saved" Moses, when he was suffering from worms; "to the astonishment" of a local doctor, Carter had also secured Pentie's complete recovery from a serious wound; he had "entirely cured" Peter of nosebleeds, where all other doctors had failed; and, in Joe's case, Carter remembered how to all appearances a shaft of lightning had struck him dead. "Yet by God's good grace," Carter reminded himself, "I alone saved and restored him."[39]

Taking care of slaves took its toll on Carter. One day he rode out "to unbend" his mind "from this prodigeous concern" of caring for slaves. The death of his "poor little slave [child] Charlotte" obviously upset him, as did that of "poor Eve" who screamed out before she died. On other occasions, the death of a slave led him to question his prescriptions and to justify his actions.[40] The psychic toll is suggested by his response to the flight of those nine slaves to the British. Both he and his daughter dreamed about them. In the father's case, he imagined them "most wretchedly meager and wan," begging him to intercede for a pardon on their behalf. Carter could not easily cast off his role as protector and guide, even when his charges had repudiated him.[41]

A more caring attitude toward slaves was no doubt shaped by Carter's confrontation with a rich family life in his slave quarters. After all, it was much easier to accord a common humanity to slaves, when they shared a family life recognizable to their masters. The master of Sabine Hall was certainly a keen observer of his slaves' family history. His awareness might take a medical form. When a slave named Daniel died, Carter recalled that he was the son of George Ball's Adam and his own Mary Adam of Ring's Neck who together had five children. Four had taken after their father and died suddenly about the age of thirty-five; the other took after her mother and was still alive. Carter detected another family pattern in that of his carpenter McGinis. His wife and their three children were, according to Carter, hypochondriacs, for "any little complaint fills them with the Apprehensions of death."[42] Resistance also ran in families—or so it seemed to Carter. At least five of Manuel's sons and daughters ran away on six separate occasions between 1770 and 1776. In 1773 Manuel even rescued his daughter Sarah after she had been captured; three years later, when Manuel ran away to Lord Dunmore, his son Billy accompanied him in order "to please his father"; and three of his other sons attempted to get away from their plantations, while their father "was contriving to get off more." What was particularly galling to Carter was that he had "obliged" Manuel many years before by facilitating the union that produced all these troublesome children. Manuel had taken a fancy to a woman named Sukey from a distant quarter; Carter brought her to Sabine Hall to become Manuel's wife.[43] Drinking also seemed to run in families: Nat and Talbot proved fond of liquor, much like their father Nassau. Finally, Carter must have been aware of a significant naming pattern among his slave families. At least four of them named sons for fathers.[44]

Carter did more than recognize slave genealogy; he understood that families mattered to slaves. He knew that slaves grieved. In 1758 he noted that his maid Winny, married to Joe, was gradually overcoming her sickness "although affected with the death of her child."[45] He knew that kin networks were important to runaways. Lansdowne old Tom learned of the whereabouts of two runaways from his wife's grandson; and a sister-in-law of one of the absentees was responsible for harboring them.[46] Carter knew that Nassau was a patriarch in his own right. Jesse, a slave belonging to John Carter, formed a liaison with one of Nassau's daughters; apparently, he kept in her father's good graces by supplying him with liquor. Conversely, Nassau returned favors to his kin, so that, when his son-in-law became sick, he cared for him in his own room.[47] Carter knew that family connections were important in job allocations. Postilion Tom was reluctant to work in Carter's garden because he did not wish to replace his father-in-law, Gardiner Johnny.[48] Slave women could impose on Carter, claiming light workloads when pregnant. One slave woman was "full 11 months before she was brought to bed."[49] Carter also experienced the wrath of a grandmother angry at the alleged mistreatment of her grandchild. The "old Granny" took her revenge by turning loose all Carter's cattle. According to her master, "she has had the impudence to say the child is poor and starved," a direct challenge to Carter's self-image of provider.[50]

The deeper one penetrates incidents like these, the more Carter seems at odds with the traditional patriarchal mode of domination. He could be severe and rigid, but he was also capable of invoking a shared humanity between master and slave. "[A]s a human creature," he said of one of his sick slaves, "I had all imaginable care taken of him." When told that his sick slaves were mending, he could "hope in God they are; for though they can be no loss to such an advanced age [Carter was sixty-one at the time], Yet they are human creatures and my soul I hope delighteth in releiving them." He could, as we have seen, "beg," "pray," and talk "a great deal . . . in most religious and affection-ate way" with a slave in order to effect a reformation of character. He could recognize that a slave mother might be "affected" by the death of her child. He could be the "forgiving" father, par-doning a fellow "creature out of humanity, religion, and every virtuous duty."[51] In these, and in many other ways, the master of Sabine Hall seems to be anticipating the more sentimental appeal to feelings that characterized masters in the nineteenth century.

II

Henry Laurens began to build up his plantations in the early 1760s. His individual units were fewer, much larger, and more self-contained than those of Carter's; but, over time, his planta-

tion operations also took on a rather dispersed character. At its
hub lay, not a rural, but, rather, an urban seat, for Laurens
directed his affairs largely from Charleston. About thirty miles
due north, in the lower part of the parish of St. John's Berkeley
lay his most important plantation, Mepkin, to which Laurens
eventually retired in the mid-1780s. About seventy miles from
Mepkin, but thirty miles northeast of Charleston, lay Wambaw
plantation in the parish of St. James Santee. This site represented
Laurens's first venture into planting; with the aid of forty to fifty
working hands, he operated it from 1756 to 1769. By the
mid-1760s, Laurens had turned his attentions southward, and
soon had settled four plantations: Broughton Island, New Hope,
Wright's Savannah, and Turtle River. The nearest of these estates
was a two-day ride or one-day sail from Charleston. By the 1770s,
he employed around two hundred slaves on these southerly plantations and another sixty or so at Mepkin and Charleston. Completing this extensive empire, Mount Tacitus, some seventy miles
north of Charleston in the Santee region, became a major indigo
estate, taken over for a time by Laurens's only surviving son.[52]

Henry Laurens, like Carter, mentioned about 180 slaves by
name: 147 he owned (in only two cases is it unclear whether
slaves with the same name were one or two persons), and 35
belonged to others. Partly as a result of the way we learn of these
slaves (via correspondence, account books, and the like, not
introspective diaries) but more because Laurens was at some
remove from their personal management, most are mentioned
only briefly. Often the reference is no more than the name of a
slave sent to one or another plantation. From the surviving
record, only about 5 slaves had relatively close contact with
Henry Laurens.[53]

One who falls into this category was Laurens's body servant,
Scipio. Before the fall of 1771, when Scipio accompanied his
master to England, he is somewhat of a shadowy figure. We catch
glimpses of him traveling back and forth between Laurens's various plantations and Charleston, taking messages and delivering

essential supplies.[54] Once in England, he comes into clearer focus. Apparently, on his own initiative, he changed his name to Robert Scipio Laurens. He and Laurens's son James shared the experience of being inoculated against smallpox; he traveled about England on his own delivering messages; he "rambl[ed] . . . in the Fields" with the master's children; he accompanied young James on his holidays; he saw to callers while Laurens wrote letters home. He was, in short, a valued member of the household. "No Stranger," Laurens observed, "could serve me so acceptably as [Robert] can." Sharing so much together, Laurens came to know Robert's personal habits, even his "grunting according to his way" as he moved about the kitchen.[55]

Predictably, this relationship did not always run smoothly. For every time we hear of Robert "behaving well," we also hear of a misdemeanor. Much like Landon Carter, Laurens can claim to "have been particularly Indulgent by exempting [his body servant] from punishment for Capital faults, from a Consideration of Instances of past Merits admitted, & the security of his own promises of amendment." Apparently, Laurens brought Robert "to England in consequence of his *own* Intreaties, founded upon his *own* apprehensions that he Should not be So well used if I left him behind me, & ten Thousand promises of attachment & good behaviour." Much like Nassau, Robert's frailties continued to be exposed. The denouement came when Robert stole some bacon which, as Laurens pointed out, "a Negro counts a Crime, to be cancelled by a flogging." Unfortunately for Robert, the burglary occurred in England, and not South Carolina. Liable to a hanging or transportation to the West Indies, the life of "foolish Rascally Robert" seemed set fair to end "in deep Tragedy." Laurens's last words on Robert reflect his disillusionment: "he is a sad Rascal, unprincipled, ungrateful, & never will be better."[56]

Stepney was another valued house servant who performed important ancillary duties for Laurens. In 1765, for instance, Laurens lent the Mepkin overseer "old Stepney" so that he might "assist in turning & watching the new Indigo." Laurens described him as "very honest," noting to the overseer that "if you will speak to him he will not allow anybody within his sight to rob you." A "half dram and a Little Toddy" were to be Stepney's daily reward. As it happened, Stepney did "not seem very willing to be from home," so Laurens ordered him back to Charleston before the month was out. Three years later, when writing to a former partner of his father's who had retired to England in 1755, Laurens passed on the important news that "Old Stepney the Drunken honest Old Fellow is still alive. Tho too often he gets dead drunk, he is our principal hand in the Garden. I have lately had his Picture drawn. He tells you how d'ye from his heart."[57] Perhaps Laurens wished to have his slave's image to take with him to England.

When Laurens was in England in the early 1770s, he made occasional inquiries of Stepney. Learning of his slave's fall from grace, Laurens reminisced on their frequent conversations in which he had predicted just such an eventuality. Even then, Laurens could not refrain from extending both his "Duty . . . and a Drink of Grog" to Stepney. On another occasion, Laurens's children passed on their greetings: "how d'y'e to old Daddy Stepney," they choroused. And when Laurens returned to Charleston in 1774, who should be there to greet him but three of his "old Domestics" (foremost among them, Stepney) who:

> drew tears from me by their humble & affectionate Salutes & congratulations my Knees were Clasped, my hands kissed my very feet embraced & nothing less than a very, I can't say fair, but *full* Buss of my Lips would satisfy the old Man [Stepney] weeping & Sobbing in my Face—the kindest enquiries over & over again were made concerning Master Jacky Master Harry Master Jemmy—they encircled me held my hands hung upon me I could scarcely get from them—Ah said the old Man I never thought to see you again, now I am happy—Ah, I never thought to see you again.

Laurens, as much as he tried to make a joke about the "fair" kiss on his lips, was obviously moved. He finally broke his "way through these humble sincere *friends* thanking them a thousand times for such marks of their affection & proceeded to Broad Street." Apart from occasional lapses into drunkenness, Stepney seems to have served quite faithfully thereafter.[58]

As this last relationship indicates, Laurens, like Carter, adopted a respectful attitude toward his more elderly slaves. Apart from Stepney, two others merit attention. One was "Old Cudjoe," a slave Laurens hired from the Reverend Richard Clarke in 1763, because he had "been used to the care of [a group of] Negroes" acquired by Laurens. Seven years later, a grateful master offered an assessment of this hired servant:

> a quiet orderly old Man, not able to do much Work and therefore is never drove to Labour, but suffer'd to go on in his own way. I observe he makes larger Crops of Rice and Corn for himself than the most able Young Negroes, which I believe is greatly owing to their Aid for they all Respect and Love him. I give him more Cloaths and Shoes than is given to any other Negro, and he seems to be so perfectly satisfied with his Situation that I believe he has no Desire to change it.

Particularly noteworthy in this testimonial is not just Laurens's manifest appreciation for this "orderly" slave's services, but the assistance given the old man by the "Young Negroes" (reminiscent of Jack Lubbar's relationship with younger slaves).[59]

The second was a slave named Cuffy, apparently a shoemaker by trade. By 1769, Laurens had other tasks in mind for "old Cuffy." He appointed him to the overseership of New Hope plantation in Georgia under the supervision of a white manager. Three years later, Cuffy elicited a glowing testimonial from his master, now resident in London. "The disposition of Old Cuffy was kind & wise," Laurens noted in a letter to his brother. "Do write that old Man by some proper means a line of comfort," he continued. By contrast, Laurens described the overseer at neighboring Broughton Island plantation as "wretched" and "not the tythe in virtue of that Black Man. Poor old Cuffy." Laurens planned to reward Cuffee when he returned to Carolina. In later years, Cuffee fell from favor, leaving Laurens "sorry to find that there was no body to interpose on his behalf." In 1778 John Lewis Gervais wrote Laurens to tell him that he had sold "Dr. Cuffee" to a backcountry planter.[60]

Laurens's relationship to skilled slaves was riven with ambivalence. Consider Sam, a mulatto bricklayer, purchased in Charleston for the large sum of £1,200 in April 1764. Over the next few years, Sam's skills as a bricklayer and woodworker were put to good use: he worked in town on hire, bringing his wages to his new master; he put up indigo vats at Mepkin; he assisted the Mepkin overseer; he put up slave chimneys made of clay; he made collars for ploughs: he relayed valuable messages between various plantations and Charleston. In 1766 Laurens described Sam as "a sensible & good fellow," and treated him to special rations.[61]

But, once Laurens had left South Carolina in 1771, disturbing reports surfaced about Sam's "ungrateful Behavior." To counter Sam's "foolish[ness]," Laurens contemplated sending Sam "and all his Boys" to Altamaha in Georgia where "the Rum . . . will not hurt him." And yet still Sam produced good work. In 1772 he put up buildings and a new rice pounding machine at Wright's Savannah. In the following year, the "New Woodpecker Machine" he built at Mepkin "exceed[ed] all Expectations." Word reached Laurens that Sam was "very clever at his work . . . & kept quite Sober." Sam wished this last piece of information to be particularly conveyed to his master, whereupon Laurens promised to write his slave a personal letter. But in 1774 "Poor Sam" had once again relapsed. He will "play the Fool in Charles Town," observed Laurens, "the place where otherwise it would best Suit his Interest & his convenience to be." The last we hear of "Sam and his boys" is in 1778, when they were repairing brick tenements in town.[62]

But perhaps nothing epitomizes better the ambivalent relationship most masters had toward their skilled slaves than Lau-

rens's capsule sketch of his native-born slave, Abraham, a man
who at the age of thirty-five possessed many talents, but not
always ones that would endear him to his master:

His good qualities SOBER.	His bad Ones
A very good boatman.	He will deceive you as often as he can.
A very good hand at the Whip Saw or any other Plantation Business.	Will pilfer trifles but always carefully keeps out of greater scrapes.
A Jobbing Carpenter so far as to thorough work & to be a great assistant to a better hand.	Fond of Women.
A tolerable good Cooper can White wash & do little plaster work.	Ungrateful & disobedient to any Man that uses him well and does not keep him close to work.
Very active, alert and Strong when he pleases.	Will feign himself Sick when he is not so.
Very healthy in general, a good horseman, and very well acquainted all over the Province.	
Much afraid of chastisement & will exert himself to ward off Whipping if he is sure of having it in case he fails.	

This balance sheet graphically portrays what many masters felt
about their artisans. Incidentally, this biography was not for
Laurens's edification alone; rather, it was intended to be useful to
the person handling Abraham's sale. Perhaps it should not surprise us that Laurens changed his mind, and Abraham continued
in his service.[63]

How can we characterize the patriarchal disposition in Laurens's case? In many ways, it was similar to Landon Carter's.
Laurens looked upon his slaves as "poor Creatures who look up to
their Master as their Father, their Guardian, & Protector, & to

whom their is a reciprocal obligation upon the Master." These obligations were various. "There is nothing of more importance," Laurens told one of his overseers, "than the care of Sick Negroes." The major difference with Carter, however, is that Laurens tended to exhort from afar. He even used the more impersonal hospitals that sprang up in Charleston and the neighboring countryside rather than trust to his overseers. In 1772, for instance, he paid two doctors the large sum of £82 for curing Claudius (an African purchased eight years earlier) of "Venereal Disorders" in their hospital.[64] "There is no part of your last letter . . . that affects me so much," Laurens told Ralph Izard, "as the want of clothing for the Negroes." When winter clothing was slow to arrive, Laurens's "heart ache[d]" for his slaves; or he found it "really shocking" that his bondmen might go barefoot.[65] When a neighboring plantation had so few provisions that "its negroes [would not] have a bite after next Sunday," Laurens was "moved" by the news and scraped together enough to last them the rest of the season.[66] In return for this solicitude, slaves were supposed to act dutifully. Thus, Laurens once told his brother, then resident in London, that his female slaves "desire[d] their Duty" to him. Laurens himself often made rewards contingent on the good behavior of his slaves.[67]

This patriarchal compact was nowhere better revealed than in a moment of crisis; and what larger crisis was there in the eighteenth century than the Revolutionary war? One Saturday evening in June 1775, Laurens called his brother's slaves together and

> admonished them to behave with great circumspection in this dangerous times, set before the great risque of exposing themselves to the treachery of pretended friends & false witnesses if they associated with any Negroes out of [his brother's] family or mine—Poor Creatures they were sensibly affected, & with many thanks promised to follow my advice & to accept the offer of my Protection.[68]

The bargain was fully explicated here: warnings and an offer of protection on the one side, promises and an acceptance of protection on the other. At the center stood the awe-inspiring, but solicitous *paterfamilias*—or so he liked to think.

Or consider a minor crisis. Frederic, one of Laurens's slaves, ran away, probably during the Revolutionary war itself. He may well have accompanied the British to New York, for in 1785 Laurens employed Jacob Read, then in the city, to recover his slave. In July Laurens wrote Read that "Frederic has already been informed I entertain no resentment against him for past faults." But Laurens was hardly in a forgiving mood:

> His apology for not returning is an additional lie. His wife was unfaithful to him only in refusing to accompany him in flight from a Master who had ever treated them both well. [T]he pretended dread of seeing his fellow servants must arise from pride, some of them who had attempted to dissuade him from deserting, at the same time predicted, "Master will certainly get you back again." [H]e is afraid to face and be laughed at by these.

Another version of the patriarchal compact was on display: the master alternating forgiveness, self-righteousness, and stern admonitions, the slave seemingly apologetic, afraid, but presumably still rebellious. In September, after Frederic's forced return, Laurens felt moved to assure Read that "I feel no kind of satisfaction from any prospect of pecuniary benefit to result from the acquisition." Frederic was not in fact "earning his Victuals," and Laurens was in a quandary whether to introduce this rebel "among his old fellow servants who are now a happy orderly family" or to sell him, thereby "increas[ing] the number of slaves." For the moment, Laurens assumed a resigned air, his slave no more than "a burthen" to him.[69]

In his reference to Frederic's good treatment, Laurens indicated that his concern for slaves went beyond mere protection. Laurens desired his overseers not just to guard but to "take care of," "be kind to" his slaves. When an overseer made it clear that he did not like a particular slave, Laurens enjoined him to remember that "he is a human Creature whether you like him or not." Indeed, Laurens insisted that his slaves be treated with "Humanity." Recalling his own actions toward a slave, Laurens emphasized that he had "treated him with all that humanity which a Man for his own Sake ought to extend to every Criature in Subjection to him."[70] A prospective separation of some of his slave families led Laurens to make an uncharacteristic outburst: "Slaves are still human Creatures," he exclaimed, "& I cannot be deaf to their cries least a time should come when I should cry & there shall be none to pity me."[71] Late in life, Laurens took great pride in his various labor-saving experiments that reduced the arduousness of his slaves' labor. These "improvements," he maintained, "are the pleasure of my life, more particularly as they contribute to bring my poor blacks to a level with the happiest peasants to be found in Europe"—a refrain that would echo down the corridors of Southern history. Conversely, slaves were expected to be faithful, even grateful for their master's solicitude. With pride, Laurens noted in the summer of 1776 that his slaves "to a Man are strongly attached to me . . . hitherto not one of them has attempted to desert." After the war was over, he contrasted the "faithless" behavior of his white servants with the "fidelity" of his slaves, "a very few instances excepted." As a result, he noted, "we are . . . endeavouring to reward those & make the whole happy."[72]

But there was a much harsher side to the patriarchal compact. First and most obvious, Laurens believed strongly that slaves *required* the presence of a master, or his delegate. When one of Laurens's overseers fell sick, the master put in an appearance to guard against "the depradations from the *ungoverned* Gentry around him."[73] The master, or his representative, had not only to be visible but also to "carry a steady command." The master's manner ought to exude "easy authority" or "gentle & discreet Authority." A "sullen Slut" of a slave could be "easily kept down," Laurens advised an overseer, "if you exert your Authority."[74] When demeanor alone failed, Laurens inevitably turned to force. Single out a couple of the more stubborn slaves, he recommended, and "chastise them severely." In Laurens's scheme of things, punishment ought to be accomplished "properly & with mercy"; nevertheless, "smart flogging[s]" were very much part of the master's stock-in-trade, although these whippings generally took place off stage, as it were, since Laurens either delegated this responsibility to his overseers or to the Charleston Work-house.[75] When force failed, or if a slave ran away, Laurens was quick to sell the offender. From 1765, when Laurens had his first runaway, to 1778, when the references peter out, Laurens mentions about thirty runaways, many of whom he sold. His benevolence had well-defined limits.[76]

The harshness at the very basis of all slavery, but conspicuously so in the Lowcountry, occasionally surfaces in Laurens's otherwise bland correspondence. On one occasion, it is no more than a casual reference that "Cow Skins" will not be sent the black drivers because they were "bad weapons" in their hands; switches were recommended in their place. On another, after hearing Laurens say more than once that he quit the African trade because it turned his stomach, we find him selling a small cargo, one of whom, he reports in matter-of-fact fashion, "hanged herself with a piece of small Vine which shews that her carcase was not very weighty." Finally, consider his offhand remark that a newly appointed overseer, an Indian named Johnson, would have to "behave above the rank of common Carolinian Fugitives, to save his Scalp a whole Year." Should Johnson's performance fall short, Laurens predicted, "the Blacks will drown him," just as they had Samuel Huey, the previous overseer. This startling acceptance of routine violence explains Laurens's injunction, "Never put your life in [Negroes'] power a moment. For a moment is sufficient to deprive you of it."[77]

The harshness of Lowcountry slavery was also evident in the fragility of black family life. Slavery was, of course, of more recent vintage in the Lowcountry as compared to the Chesapeake. Consequently, slave families lacked generational depth. Men far outnumbered women, so that Laurens on more than one occasion recognized the necessity of providing wives for his single adult males. But Laurens also built up his slave force extremely rapidly; he was therefore heavily reliant on imported African cargoes, two-thirds of whom were generally men. Certainly, on the few occasions when Laurens specified that purchases or groups of slaves be transferred from one plantation to another, males predominated.[78] The act of naming indicates something of the difference in the quality of family life: many of Landon Carter's slaves had assumed the right to name within their families; most of Laurens's slaves received their names from their master or other whites. At one point, Laurens thought primarily in terms of place names, so some of his bondmen ended up as *Senegal, Pondicherry,* and *Quebec;* at another, the classical muse held sway, so his slaves received names like *Othello, Tully,* and *Claudius;* perhaps a lighter, more frivolous mood accounts for his decision to retain the name *King Cole,* one supplied by a slaver's sailors, and to use the local term *Rough Rice* for two of his shipboard purchases.[79]

Families did exist on Laurens's plantations. The most direct reference, however, underlines their fragility. When Laurens's partnership with John Coming Ball came to an end in 1765, no fewer than seven or eight of his slave families were threatened with divisions of "Fathers, Mothers, Husbands, Wives & Children."[80] Significantly, Laurens mentioned close family ties. Only the immediate slave family, not extended family linkages, make an appearance in Laurens's correspondence. Thus, we hear that Cain and his son were woodworkers; that Chloe was of old Cain's family; that Liverpool and Peter were brothers; and that Scaramouch received money to purchase a coffin for his dead child.[81] Slave grandparents, cousins, uncles, and aunts are conspicuous by their absence. Even Laurens's offhand remarks suggest the pressures to which the slave family in South Carolina was subject. While in London, Laurens observed the number of petitions for divorce that came before the House of Lords; they put him in mind of "our Negroes throwing away one Wife and taking another." Laurens's attitude to slave family life tended to be utilitarian. When the governor of East Florida declined to purchase a slave woman that Laurens had acquired for him, the Carolinian derided the Scotsman's lack of understanding of "Plantation affairs." "Southern folk," Laurens observed, would know that this slave was a "breeding Woman & in ten Years time may have double her worth in her own Children." Although Laurens attempted to respect family ties among his slaves, economic calculations were never far removed.[82]

Rice cultivation, which formed the primary employment for most of Laurens's slaves, was far more arduous than the tending of tobacco. Moreover, Laurens undoubtedly kept his slaves hard at work. When relegating a slave to the field, he spoke of his future "hard Labour." He attempted to ensure that slaves worked constantly throughout the year. In the winter months, his slaves repaired dams. If they had any other "Interval of Leisure," Laurens ordered that they cut timber. Laurens could also be found advocating something like a time and motion study, not too far removed from his Chesapeake counterpart. And although South Carolina slaves worked under a different labor system from their Virginia cousins, the work was far from light. When rebellious Amy was turned to the field, Laurens told his overseer to "make her perform a task every day to keep her cool."[83]

However, tasking did have a significant advantage over ganging in that it allowed the slave a measure of latitude to determine his own work pace. Furthermore, in at least one instance, some of Laurens's slaves enjoyed lighter than usual tasks. At Wright's Savannah in 1772 the overseer was so lax in his duty that slave "Tasks [fell] Short nea[r]ly 1/5 of what they should be." Perhaps, noted Laurens's deputy, the overseer wished "to make Friends with the Negroes." Certainly, the lowcountry master was often a distant presence to his slaves, and this gave them even more room for maneuver. "[W]e are forced to trust to Negroes," lamented Laurens, "'tis impossible to be constantly with them, and they are apt to commit Blunders, and do worse Things."[84] Laurens had also to rely on slave drivers, who assumed considerable authority in his absence. One of Laurens's drivers even criticized an overseer's indigo, saying it had been "steep'd rather too long" in "Lime Water [that was] too strong." Where slaves had achieved autonomy in the workplace to this degree, they must have been able to deflect some of the drive for profits exhibited by masters. Even Laurens himself could adopt a resigned tone. Do the best you can, he once advised his brother, for those slaves who "behave ill, I shall only loose Money by."[85]

Arguably, a less intimate relationship between master and slave occurred more frequently where many bondmen were culturally alien. Landon Carter never mentioned an African slave; Laurens, on the other hand, not only purchased many, he knew the ethnic background and the "country names" of more than a few. Apparently, he knew of at least one case of an African-style marital arrangement; it came to his notice at Mepkin when one of Mathias's wives poisoned the other.[86] Although Laurens expressed little interest in his slaves' African heritage, he knew that they played an African game with a monetary unit known as "pappaa dice" and that the slave term for sesame was "Bene." Perhaps even their mode of talking rubbed off on him, if his "how d'ye"s can be attributed to them.[87]

From the slaves' point of view, a more distanced relationship with a master left them a greater measure of autonomy. Laurens's slaves engaged in more independent production than was ever possible for Chesapeake slaves. Certainly, Landon Carter never bought tobacco from his bondmen (indeed, production of tobacco was very definitely prohibited for Chesapeake slaves), whereas Henry Laurens spoke of being his slaves' "Factor," selling them cloth, hats, iron pots, "gay Wastcoats" at 7/6 a bushel, for their rice. In 1765 he advised one of his overseers to purchase provisions from the slaves "at the lowest price that they will sell it for." In 1769 he laid out L158.15 in sundries to his "Wambaw Negroes for their Rice." Four years later, he provided a variety of cloth (from oznabrugs to check, from garlix to blue plains) as well as

fine handkerchiefs, felt hat, and thread to his slaves at Wright's
Savannah, "for Rice and Corn of their Own which they sold to the
Overseers."[88] His slaves certainly owned money and property:
make them pay their own ferriages, he ordered his overseers, if
they wish to come to town to make complaints; see that "all their
Little Estates [are] packed up," assure them that "each Man's
property shall be safely deliver'd," he demanded, when transfer-
ring slaves from one plantation to another.[89]

III

Thomas Thistlewood arrived in Jamaica in 1750. For twelve
months, he worked as an estate manager at Vineyard cattle pen in
St. Elizabeth parish in the southwest part of the island; he then
graduated to the overseership of Egypt sugar estate, located near
Savannah La Mar in adjoining Westmoreland parish; after sixteen
years in that position, during which time he began to acquire
slaves and property, he set up his own provisioning estate, Bread-
nut Island Pen, within sight of his former residence. He lived out
the remainder of his life by selling produce locally and hiring out
his jobbing gang of about thirty slaves. Although never a promi-
nent slaveowner, he worked on large estates and had the command of large numbers of slaves. Thistlewood's life can provide
valuable insights into the relationship of master and slaves.[90]

In his daily journal, which extends for the thirty-six years he
lived in Jamaica, Thistlewood named well over a thousand slaves.
This huge number owes something to the scale of Thistlewood's
reportage but much more to the size of Jamaican estates and to
the absence of white companions. On January 8, 1751, for instance, Thistlewood noted that he had not seen a white face since
December 19.[91] Thistlewood was surrounded by blacks; his most
intense and recurrent contacts were with them; he lived in a
predominantly black world.

Thistlewood, like many another Jamaican planter and overseer,
took a black mistress. At first, he had sexual encounters with a
variety of slave women. In his first six months at Vineyard, he
recorded sleeping with five slaves, three of whom were certainly

Africans, on twenty-five separate occasions. In his first year at
Egypt, he slept with eleven women, seven of whom were Africans (five Ibos), on fifty-three occasions. But, by the middle of
his second year—mid-July 1753, to be exact—Thistlewood began
to have sex with a housemaid named Phibbah, and gradually
settled into a relatively monogamous union with her. Certainly,
Thistlewood still had sex with other women, which often led to
quarrels with Phibbah (and more than one dose of the clap); and
he, on more than one occasion, voiced suspicions about her
fidelity. In actual fact, the two of them seem to have had rather
unorthodox sexual attitudes, for Thistlewood once mentioned
having sex with a slave while Phibbah was in the same bed; she,
in turn, procured a "sweetheart," one "Mountain Lucy," for him
when she gave birth. Despite various tiffs, the two of them
obviously had a passionate relationship (in January 1755, a quite
typical month, Thistlewood recorded having sex twenty-one
times with Phibbah, once each with three other slave women).[92]

The relationship went deeper than mere sexual attraction. One
Sunday evening, Thistlewood and an extremely pregnant Phibbah took a stroll together; Thistlewood visited Phibbah every day
after she had given birth to a stillborn child; and the two of them
went fishing after she regained her strength. It was a relatively
evenhanded relationship for a master and a slave. Thistlewood
gave Phibbah small gifts of clothing, a large English-made knife, a
sea chest, and the like; she gave him a pineapple, a puppy,
saltfish, and handmade nightcaps. On more than one occasion,
she refused to come to him at night, or would not talk to him all
day, or removed her effects from his house, or damned him to his
face. Nor was Phibbah without a measure of economic independence: Thistlewood mentioned her various plots of ground; she
possessed at least one horse, some hogs, and fowl; and she earned
money by selling handmade items of clothing and the produce
from her grounds.[93]

The summer of 1757 put their relationship to the test.
Thistlewood had a disagreement with his employer and left Egypt

to seek new employ a day's ride away. At their parting, Phibbah gave Thistlewood "a gold ring to keep for her sake." Over the next few days, she bombarded him with gifts: a fine land turtle, biscuits, cheese, bread, mudfish, and naseberries. One week after his departure, Phibbah visited Thistlewood on the weekend. This occasion, and many similar ones over the next few months, were times of torrid lovemaking. Sundays allowed Thistlewood to show his lover around his new estate, while she brought him up to date with the week's happenings at Egypt. On Mondays, Phibbah generally borrowed his horse to ride back to Egypt, he provided a slave escort because dangerous woods had to be negotiated, and she left a forlorn Thistlewood lonely at her absence. Over the next few months, more goods—a large pumpkin, cushoes, crabs, turtle eggs, baskets, pineapples, soap, rice, eels, potatoes, vinegar, jerked pork, okra, yams, two young dogs, even a young sow—arrived from Phibbah, while Thistlewood expressed his gratitude and sent plantains, pineapples, even roses to her. Meanwhile, Thistlewood learned that Phibbah was ill, which provoked a rare outburst against "miserable slavery." Finally, Thistlewood's former employer sent a conciliatory letter, shrewdly entrusting it to Phibbah, that eventually effected a reconciliation. After a six-month absence, Thistlewood returned to Egypt, his relationship with Phibbah firmly cemented.[94] She was his "wife"; she eventually bore him a son and lived with him until his death, whereupon she received a handsome bequest and her freedom in his will. Truly, this was an intense relationship between master and slave.

Thistlewood had a remarkably cooperative relationship with an elderly slave named Sharper, who belonged to Mrs. Anderson, a resident of Westmoreland parish. In June 1750, before he took up his position at Vineyard, Thistlewood traveled about the Westmoreland plain. He visited a plantain walk at which Sharper, a watchman, resided. Described as "a Clever old fellow" and a "Sensible Negro," Sharper made a favorable impression on Thistlewood. He enhanced this impression by introducing the visitor to a number of native dishes—"pepper pot" (a soup made from cassava roots) and "tum tum" (a Twi word referring to a dish made, in Sharper's case, from mashed or pounded plantain and fish). When Thistlewood moved back to Westmoreland in 1751, Sharper became one of his charges. The watchman's hut stood about three-quarters of a mile from the Egypt plantation house, so the two met infrequently. However, the contacts were almost always cordial and constructive. In March 1753, for instance, Sharper shaved Thistlewood for money; in August of the following year, Thistlewood began buying a "diet drink" from Sharper that promised relief for the clap (since Thistlewood's doses were frequent, the trickle of money into Sharper's pocket was fairly constant). Sharper also performed useful duties of a non-pecuniary nature. He made baskets for the Egypt slaves; he captured and brought home a number of runaways; he rowed the canoe in which Thistlewood went fishing. Sharper was a trusted and respected elderly slave.[95]

Sugar plantations were factories in the field; to get the job done, Thistlewood, like any manager of a sugar estate, relied on skilled slave labor. To pick at random just one slave, let us follow one year out of the life of Quashe, a mason who worked at the Egypt mill. Quashe's skills were valued by Thistlewood, and he was quick to reward the artisan for good work. Quashe usually received extra rations—perhaps a half-dozen mackerel, a bottle of rum, a parcel of sugar. Consequently, Quashe acquired property. Thistlewood once shot one of Quashe's hogs which had strayed into the "corn piece." One Sunday in 1752 saw master and slave exchanging gifts: Sharper offered taya (the Jamaican creole word for the coco plant) and calalu (a cabbage-like plant); Thistlewood reciprocated with rum and sugar.

Aside from these mutually respectful contacts, the two played out a number of contests throughout the year. But at Christmas time a major confrontation arose. The end of the year was always a nervous time: the slaves were often worked hard before the holidays; the festivities themselves often loosened restraints and occasionally turned violent; and a manager's annual contract was eligible for renewal. To compound matters, two days after Christmas, Thistlewood chanced to encounter a runaway, Congo Sam, on a local road. A ferocious struggle took place, in which Thistlewood, with the aid of his pimento walking stick, only just managed to ward off the cut and thrust of Sam's machete. Eventually, master overcame rebel; Thistlewood held his captive in an armlock and waited for help. Two of his slave women came by, but, after conversing with Sam in their native language—an occurrence that made Thistlewood "much afraid of them"—they refused to offer assistance. But, fortunately for Thistlewood, a few more reliable slaves and some white passersby soon arrived on the scene and came to his aid. As a weary and disturbed manager reflected on the day's events, he recalled an incident that occurred just three days before Christmas. Quashe had announced "before all the Negroes that [Thistlewood] should not eat much more meat here." When Thistlewood inquired whether Quashe planned to poison or murder him, the self-assured artisan replied, "neither, but he intended to invent some great lye, and go tell his master, to get [Thistlewood] turned away." Quashe also claimed that his master "would believe a Negro before a White man." Thistlewood began to suspect that his meeting with Congo Sam was no chance encounter. Quashe, he now believed, knew that "Sam had intended to Murder me." A few days later, Quashe received more rewards from Thistlewood for good work, the incident apparently, but surely never quite, forgotten.[96]

These quick snapshots, taken randomly from a long-running serial drama, give the flavor of Thistlewood's interactions with slaves. On the one hand, Thistlewood and the slaves under his charge shared a great deal—far more than Carter or Laurens ever did. Slaves introduced Thistlewood to the fauna and flora of the island; they provided him "mamme gum" (a substance drawn from the mammee-apple tree, similar to the sapodilla, which black doctors used against chigoes) and gongo (pigeon peas); he witnessed their dances; he heard their "Creolian, Congo and Coromantee, &c. Musick"; he listened to their musical instruments, such as drums made from gourds or the banjo (otherwise known as the "strum strum" or "merrywong," he noted); he ate their African-style dishes such as asham (taken from the Twi word 'o-siam,' meaning parched corn) and he drank out of their carved calabash bowls; he recorded their ethnic proverbs, learning about monsters in "Papua country" and strange beasts in "Coromantee"; he likened their belief in "duppies" (referring to a person's shadow, spirit, or soul) to the Yorkshire superstition about padfoots (goblins); he admired their ability to rope cattle, making sketches of their technique (and Thistlewood was an experienced stockman in his native Lincolnshire); he was even rather tickled by the names one slave gave his dogs—"Gainst Me," "Fair to my Face," "Help myself," "Creold Woman," "Good Women's Scarce," and "Women want all."[97]

Thistlewood did not, of course, have a personal stake—at least not in his first few years on the island—in the welfare of slaves. And yet the patriarchal ethos was not foreign to him. After all, he dispensed rations, tools, clothing, and medicine; he ensured order and he resolved disputes. Moreover, he acted out of more than duty. When a white man attempted to beat one of the Egypt slaves "wrongfully," Thistlewood intervened. When Quaw ran away in 1756, he was "forgiven" because it was his first offense and he "promises fair." On one occasion Thistlewood donated rum, sugar, beef, and pepper pot to a Vineyard slave woman for her housewarming. She wished to treat her fellow slaves, particularly her shipmates. Thistlewood attended the event and marvelled at the various performances of fire-eating and "Congo dancing." At his departure from Vineyard, Thistlewood handed out much of his old clothing, various household items, and food and drink to his favorite slaves. Apart from these special events, his everyday existence was punctuated by a small gift to this slave, a payment for services rendered to another, an exchange of goods to yet others. Without stretching his imagination too far, Thistlewood could envision himself as some ancient patriarch surrounded by bondmen and bondwomen.[98]

On the other hand, Thistlewood—and Jamaican slavery, in general—extended the bounds of severity inherent in patriarchalism to its very limits—and beyond. Whippings were a common occurrence. During his first year of employment, he had thirty-five slaves whipped a total of fifty-two times. The punishments were harsh, ranging from 50 to 150 lashes. And once Thistlewood acclimated to the more brutal world of a sugar estate, he stepped up the punishments and made them more sadistic. He applied face brandings, shackled slaves in bilboes, put cart chains about their necks, and rubbed salt, lime juice, and urine into their wounds. He devised particularly humiliating punishments. On some occasions, he spread molasses over a slave and exposed him to flies all day and to mosquitoes at night without benefit of a fire. For eating sugar cane, he devised "Derby's dose," whereby Derby, a slave, would defecate into a culprit's mouth, which would then be gagged shut for some hours. As might be imagined, runaways were a constant problem. During his year at the cattle pen, nine of forty-two slaves ran away at least once. Two recent African immigrants disappeared repeatedly. Several of the slaves became violent. One man hacked a woman with a cutlass, and two others pulled knives when cornered. Thistlewood inured himself to the savagery of a sugar plantation. He mellowed only when he left its rigors for the more relaxed routines of a provisioning estate.[99]

Thistlewood rarely mentioned the family life of his charges. Perhaps he viewed this as their private affair, but the omission of even tangential references does seem surprising for such an inquisitive reporter. The little he does say suggests the fragile, even chaotic, quality of family life among Jamaican slaves. Perhaps Sam brought his wife home after she had run away because he missed her; but no such charitable interpretation seems possible for Charles, who beat up Mary, a Coromantee; or for Sancho, who left his wife the same day he caught her sleeping with another slave; or Adam, who denied his wife her share of their food rations. Thistlewood made matters worse, of course, by forcing his sexual attentions on many of his slave women, although perhaps he slept so often with Africans because they were unattached. The naming of slaves also indicates the scale of white interference. Only eight slaves at Egypt plantation shared a name with another slave, while thirty-five had the dubious distinction of sharing a name with a mule or cow.[100]

Thistlewood's slaves might well imagine themselves as beasts of burden whenever they reflected on the work demanded of them. On April 10, 1752, Thistlewood noted that the sugar crop had required "63 days (almost 11 weeks) with 1189 cutters" to complete. For about three months, then, twenty or so slaves had worked six days a week at one of the most strenuous agricultural tasks known to eighteenth-century man, namely, cutting cane. Others transported the cane to the mill, where yet others ground the cane stalks well into the night, while yet others took "spells" in the boiling house reducing the canejuice to brown sugar, while yet others worked in the distillery producing rum. This was a complex, continuous, and above all intense process, for sugarcane had to be rushed from field to mill and then processed without delay, or it would spoil. The exertions required of Caribbean slaves far exceeded anything expected of their Chesapeake or lowcountry counterparts. Thistlewood mentions only three births in 1752; two children were born in the spring, and both died almost immediately. Sugar worked its deadly course on prospective as well as present generations.[101]

The work routine at Egypt plantation was not without respite. So far as one can tell, Thistlewood never worked his slaves on Sunday. The day after the crop had been harvested, he gave out rum and sugar so that the slaves might "make merry." Before that, he had passed out punch and drams of rum as encouragements to labor. During the course of the year, he allowed nine Saturdays and two Thursdays as rest days, as well as Easter and

Whitsuntide Monday and a number of days at Christmas. If this was not a relaxed routine, the work undoubtedly slackened in pace during the second half of the year, as slaves tended to the corn and plantains grown on the estate and to their own mountain provision grounds.[102]

Indeed, despite the brutalities and harshness of life at Egypt, there can be no question that Thistlewood's slaves were the most independent of the three groups under review. They obviously had a rich community life; they planted their own separate grounds; and many possessed livestock. On Sundays, Thistlewood attended the "Negro market," run by slaves, where he often bought plantains, corn, alligator pears (avocados), and other provisions for himself and the estate. A special case, no doubt, but an illuminating one nevertheless, was the property acquired by mulatto Will, an Egypt slave. On March 21, 1758, Thistlewood drew up a will or "memorandum," as he termed it, for the dying slave. Will bequeathed a cow to his wife's shipmate, a heifer to Hester, his daughter, and his filly and the balance of his estate to his wife. Will further requested that he be buried at Salt River, at his mother's right hand, and that there be no singing around his grave, as was customary.[103] It is difficult, not to say impossible, to imagine such an incident occurring in the Chesapeake, and only a little less so in the Lowcountry.

IV

The patriarchal ethos conjures up visions of "well regulated" households in which governance, adjudication, rigid control, order, and severe discipline were the dominant features. This was particularly true in a world deeply divided between powerful and privileged masters on the one hand and powerless and un-privileged slaves on the other. All three planters reveal much that supports this general view. Certainly, Thistlewood's regime was by far the most brutal; Carter's and Laurens's somewhat less so; but all three were severe patriarchs. True, the *pater* would, in the words of the seventeenth-century political theorist Robert

Filmer, generally "preserve, feed, clothe, instruct, and defend" his servants; but, as Filmer also emphasized, "Saul lost his kingdom for being too merciful."[104] Eighteenth-century masters never forgot this cautionary reminder. Carter applied the rod harshly and, in almost his last breath, called slaves "devils"; Laurens railed at individual slaves, calling them variously "a vile Scoundrell," an "eye Servant & a great Rogue," an "impudent gipsey," and was quick to sell a recalcitrant one; Thistlewood let his actions speak for him and punished savagely and sadistically.[105]

Severity from masters wrought great damage on slaves. From whippings to harsh work discipline, from broken families to cultural loss, the catalog of hardships faced by slaves is numbing in its enormity. Moreover, some slaves were drawn into a tragic complicity in their own fate. Consider, for example, an incident related by Landon Carter. He once whipped one of his son's slaves, suspected of committing a crime on one of Landon's quarters. "[I]n a most violent passion," the injured slave called Carter's humanity into question and declared that Carter "was not his master and his master would not have let him be served so." True, this slave was not submissive, and he even called Carter a murderer to his face; but his ultimate recourse was to invoke the protection of his own master. In a sense, patriarchalism could insidiously coopt even the most rebellious slave. Or, consider a slave temporarily in Laurens's care. The slave was at a loose end, unable to settle down, allowed to "do as he pleases," and ultimately "dissatisfied, . . . querulous, troublesome." The reason, Laurens pointed out to his absentee friend, was "for want of knowing who is his Master."[106] Or finally, consider the dramatic incident in the fields involving Thistlewood and Mason Quashe. This outspoken and confident slave had spoken of going to his master and informing on Thistlewood. Quashe was like a moth drawn to the light. His instincts were sound and understandable but, in order to pursue his course, he succumbed to the power of his master. An even greater sacrifice occurred when the owner of Egypt estate died a few years later. A slave named Roger, another mason, committed suicide in order "to wait upon his master in the other world." What more telling incident to underscore the tragic involvement of slaves in their own oppression![107]

In a thoroughgoing patriarchal household, the subjection of the servants was absolute and unquestioned. The master was first cause, prime mover, almost a demigod. Restraint, order, and authority were his constant watchwords. But, gradually, new values infiltrated this patriarchal citadel—again, they were most evident in Laurens's and Carter's cases, but Thistlewood was not immune to their influence. First came contractual notions that stressed the specific duties of, and restraints on, the master. Reciprocity became the dominant idiom. Following closely on its heels came a new constellation of ideas and values, revolving around a greater recognition of emotion, sentiment, and feelings. Masters began to view themselves less as harsh taskmasters grandly presiding over their estates and more as benefactors providing for their dependents. Austere, rigid patriarchalism slowly gave way to warm, mellow paternalism. Slavery would soon be viewed as a benign and protective institution; slaves would, in Fitzhugh's exaggerated words, soon be enveloped in "domestic affection"; and, before long, it would be the master for whom pity would be invoked as "the greatest slave" of all.[108] The antebellum South saw the most well developed expression of this outlook; but early nineteenth-century Jamaica, as any reader of the journals of "Monk" Lewis or Lady Nugent can attest, moved a little in the same direction.[109]

With the emphasis on reciprocity, negotiation between master and slave (however unequal the contest) became ever more commonplace. As we have seen, slaves were constantly attempting to extract some advantage, however small, from the patriarchal compact. If patriarchalism legitimized class rule, then, it could also be turned to the slaves' advantage. As we have also seen, the types of encounters played out by masters and different groups of slaves could be remarkably similar across space. Intense, expressive encounters with a few favorite house servants, respectful though never harmonious relations with elderly slaves, deeply ambivalent contacts with artisans—these are just three examples of the myriad little dramas played out between masters and dependents across plantation America. What lies at the heart of all of them, as Orlando Patterson has noted, is the struggle for advantage relentlessly pursued, "sometimes noisily, more often quietly; sometimes violently, more often surreptitiously; infrequently with arms, always with the weapons of the mind and soul."[110]

With patriarchalism gradually giving way to paternalism, an interesting paradox comes into sharper focus. The regime which probably was the least severe of the three under review (namely, Landon Carter's) was precisely the one to allow the slaves least room for independence. On the other hand, the most savage (namely, Thistlewood's) granted slaves the most autonomy, with Laurens's rule occupying a middle place between these two extremes. Within various eighteenth-century slave societies, then, one can discern a pattern that would differentiate nineteenth-century Southern slavery from its predecessors. As slavery became softer, more openly solicitous of the slave, so it became tighter, providing less room for the slave's private endeavors. If there was more brutality in eighteenth-century slavery than its successors, at least there was also more latitude for the slave. Tragedy and irony were at the heart of that inhumane institution, slavery, to the last.[111]

The Africanization of the Lowcountry Labor Force, 1670–1730

RUSSELL R. MENARD

By the middle of the eighteenth century a remarkable society was firmly rooted in the Carolina Lowcountry. Its salient characteristics included: a substantial black majority, large plantations, an impressive prosperity based on export agriculture; a broad distribution of land and slaves among white households; and a powerful ruling class, rapidly gaining in confidence and self-consciousness, eager to control the colony's development.[1]

The most striking characteristic was the black majority, which made the region "more like a negro country than like a country settled by white people."[2] Slaves were a majority in South Carolina as early as 1708, although a substantial number of them were Indians and the black and white populations were roughly equal. By 1740, slaves—then almost all black—were more than 70 percent of the total (Table 1). The Stono revolt of 1739 joined with a severe depression during King George's War (1739–1748) nearly to eliminate slave imports during the 1740s. In consequence, the black population fell to just over 60 percent of the total at mid-century, still high by mainland standards. That figure, furthermore, includes Charleston, where blacks were only about half the total, and the growing backcountry settlements, where slaves were rare. In the Lowcountry plantation districts the black population was much larger, perhaps 80 percent of the whole.[3]

The large size of Lowcountry plantations and the great wealth of their owners is also striking. It is clearly documented in tax lists and probate records. A partial tax list taken in 1745 for St. James Goose Creek Parish provides illustration. It reports an average of 43 slaves and 2400 acres of taxable land per household. Only two of the 59 households on the list owned no slaves, while 16 reported more than 50 and 5 over 100. The three largest planters, Henry Izard, James Kinloch, and Sara Middleton, owned on average 220 slaves, 11,000 acres of land, and £3500 sterling in money at interest. Again by mainland standards, these were big businesses.[4]

South Carolina's black majority and large plantations produced export crops, chiefly rice and indigo, which earned high incomes for Lowcountry whites. Over the years 1768 to 1772, exports per capita from South Carolina averaged £3.7 sterling, more than three times the figure for the remaining mainland colonies.[5] High export earnings led to impressive wealth levels. Mean movable wealth per decedent doubled between 1740 and 1760 and grew at an even faster rate in the next fifteen years. In 1774, Lowcountry decedents were worth on average £2700 sterling, over six times the figure for the thirteen colonies as a whole.[6] On the eve of the Revolution, South Carolina, if not "the most thriving Country perhaps on this Globe," was at least "the most oppulent and flourishing colony on the British Continent of America."[7]

The Lowcountry's black majority, large plantations, and impressive wealth are well-known, among the staples of the historical literature on British America. The fourth characteristic, the broad distribution of land and slaves, is less familiar. Simply put, the great majority of white household heads owned both land and slaves. The widespread ownership of slaves is clearly established by probate inventories: in most years from the 1720s to the 1760s more than three-quarters of the decedents owned slaves, while among those who earned their income from agriculture that proportion was greater than 95 percent. The evidence on land is less firm, but it describes a similarly wide distribution.[8] The Lowcountry lacked a large class of tenants and slaveless yeomen farmers. It was, to a degree seldom achieved elsewhere in the Americas, a republic of slaveholders, a fact of great political consequence.

The Lowcountry's black majority, large plantations, great wealth, and broad distribution of land and slaves are easily established. The fifth characteristic, an indigenous, powerful, and responsible ruling class, is a matter of interpretation, and much more controversial. While no one questions the power of the great planters, some doubt their cohesion, others their responsibility, stressing instead their self-indulgent individuality and arguing that they lacked the sense of collectivity, stewardship, and accomplishment, the commitment to the colony's future, one expects of an effective ruling class. Such a view reflects a misunderstanding of their role in local government and in the development of the backcountry and rests on inappropriate comparisons to the Chesapeake gentry who ruled in a very different context. While a detailed assessment is beyond the scope of this essay, the character of the great planters is clearly revealed during the Revolution. In that era a vision of a slaveholder's republic nurtured by their Lowcountry accomplishments, persuaded them to risk a comfortable position within the old empire to pursue a passionately held, if perverse, prospect of a new empire in America.[9]

It was not any one of these characteristics that made the Lowcountry unique. Most of the sugar islands had a black majority, large plantations, and wealthy whites, while Barbados at least combined those features with a broad distribution of land and slaves.[10] Other American colonies, Virginia for example, were governed by a powerful indigenous ruling class eager to seize power and build a new republican future.[11] But only the Lowcountry possessed all those characteristics in combination. If we are to understand Lowcountry society—and, more broadly, the range of social configurations possible in the Americas—we must come to grips with the origins of its unique plantation regime.[12]

That regime arose in the early decades of the eighteenth century in a set of tightly interconnected transformations that thoroughly reshaped South Carolina society. Between 1670 and 1730 South Carolina shifted from a mixed economy to one dominated

by rice, from a region of small farms to one dominated by plantations, and from a diverse labor force to one dominated by African
slaves. Within the severe constraints imposed by the poor quality
of the evidence, this essay explores those transformations, focusing on the process basic to them all, the growth of Carolina's black
majority, in an effort to understand the origins of the Lowcountry
plantation system.

The Issue

With the advantage of hindsight, there is an air of the inevitable
to the rise of African slavery in South Carolina. By the middle of
the eighteenth century Africans, slavery, and Lowcountry plantations had become so thoroughly entwined as to seem inseparable.
The identification of blacks and bondage was in the end so powerful and African slavery was eventually so central a feature of
Carolina society that it takes a major effort of historical imagination to entertain other outcomes. That effort is essential, for
neither the Africanization of slavery nor its entrenchment in the
Lowcountry was inevitable. "The Africanization of large parts of
the New World," David Brion Davis argues, "was the result not of
concerted planning, racial destiny, or immanent historical design
but of innumerable local and pragmatic choices made in four
continents."[13] That statement is as true for the particular case of
the Carolina Lowcountry as it is for America as a whole.

As Peter Wood notes, "alternative sources of labor were very
real possibilities during the early years of Lowland settlement."[14]
In the seventeenth century South Carolina's labor force consisted
of a mixture of free and indentured white workers from Great
Britain, Indians purchased, captured, or hired from neighboring
tribes, and black slaves brought from the West Indies, chiefly
Barbados. By the 1720s, this polygot work force had been sub-
merged under a floodtide of African slaves. At one level, the
sources of this transition are clear. Before 1700 the mixed labor
force served the needs of local landowners. The South Carolina
economy was based on subsistence farming, a provisions and

timber trade to the West Indies, and furs, and the labor demands of the export sector were small. Then, in the early decades of the eighteenth century, the production of naval stores boomed and rice culture spread through the lowlands, the demand for workers increased, old sources of supply proved inadequate, and the South Carolina labor force was soon overwhelmingly African.[15]

While the outline of the story is clear enough, the details are still murky and several mysteries remain. Why did South Carolinians not rely on slaves brought directly from Africa from the start? A major trade in slaves to the West Indies was well-established by the colony's founding. Surely it would have been a simple matter to divert an occasional ship to the Lowcountry. Why did free workers, servants, and Indians prove inadequate once the economy boomed? Surely more workers could have been lured from Britain's numerous poor or captured in America's vast interior. We can gain some insight into these questions by looking more closely at the shifting composition of the Lowcountry work force, the changing labor demands of the Carolina economy, and the supply of workers available from various sources.

The Composition of the Lowcountry Work Force, 1670–1730

Estimates made by local officials reveal the structure of Carolina's population at the beginning of the eighteenth century, in 1703 and 1708 (Table 2). White servants were only a minor part of the unfree work force, numbering 200 in 1703, less than 3 percent of the total population and 6 percent of the bound workers. Over the next five years, some servants died or gained their freedom and few arrived to take their place. Their number fell, to only 120, roughly 1 percent of the total and 2 percent of the unfree laborers. Slaves, on the other hand, increased markedly over the period. The Lowcountry was already a slave society in 1703, when its 3,000 blacks and 350 Indians made up 47 percent of the population. Between 1703 and 1708 the white population, battered by "the Late sickness" and held down by the "small supply from other parts," barely held its own, rising from 3,800 to 4,080. The colony gained 1,100 blacks, however, through natural increase and from the West Indies, and 1,050 Indian slaves "by reason of our late conquest over the French and Spaniards and the success of our forces against the Appallackys and other Indian engagements."[16] In 1708 there were 5,500 slaves in the Lowcountry, 4,100 of them black, 1,400 Indian, accounting for 57 percent of the total population.

No similarly comprehensive data remain for earlier or later years, but a combination of tax lists, parish census records, *post-mortem* inventories, and contemporary observations permit a description of the work force in 1730. The message of these data is clear: the Lowcountry work force was overwhelmingly enslaved, black, and African. South Carolina's population was two-thirds enslaved in 1730, and only a handful were Indians. There were few indentured servants and free white workers, most of them craftsmen or overseers on the larger plantations. And the composition of the black population had changed as West Africa replaced the sugar islands as the major source of new slaves.[17]

Data for the seventeen century are scarce, but it is clear that Carolina had a much different work force early in its history. Records of headrights—warrants for land awarded to immigrants—are full of pitfalls for the historian, and those of Carolina seem especially problematic. Nevertheless, they provide precious clues to the composition of the labor force during the seventeenth century. In the 1670s, servants outnumbered slaves among new arrivals by more than 6 to 1, while white immigrants outnumbered blacks by 13 to 1 (Table 3). White servants were the major source of unfree labor during the initial decade of the English occupation of the Lowcountry.[18]

There were, then, these data suggest, two major transformations in the Carolina work force during the first half century. The first, completed by 1703, was a shift from servitude to slavery. The second, finished in the 1720s, was a transition from blacks from the West Indies and Native American slaves to a work force drawn increasingly from West Africa.[19] We can gain insight into these shifts through a close examination of the Lowcountry labor market, by surveying the changing supply of servants, Indians, and blacks, and by assessing the demand for workers among South Carolina planters.[20]

The First Transition: From Servants to Slaves

By the time the first permanent English settlement was established in the Lowcountry, colonizers were able to draw on more than a half-century of experience in developing British America. All the English colonies faced the problem of recruiting a labor force, and a variety of methods and populations had been tried. Indentured servitude represented one of the more successful and enduring responses. By 1670 it had played a central role in the development of the British West Indies and the Chesepeake colonies, accounting for perhaps 85 percent of the white migration to those regions and financing the Atlantic passage of roughly 150,000 settlers to English America as a whole. Not surprisingly, the promoters of South Carolina anticipated that indentured servants would supply a major share of the colony's work force and they took steps to organize their recruitment immediately.[21]

Their timing was unfortunate, for the days when servants willingly left England in numbers sufficient to the needs of colonial planters had already passed. British migration to America peaked in the 1650s and then declined, largely in response to falling population and improved opportunities at home. Carolinians recruited among a diminishing supply of willing migrants and they did so in the face of increased competition from other colonial regions, particularly the sugar islands and the tobacco coast but also from William Penn's new colony in the mid-Atlantic area.[22]

While all colonial regions felt the pinch, paid the higher prices, and offered the shorter terms that the new conditions required, Lowcountry planters labored under some particular disadvantages. For one thing, the colony quickly developed a reputation as a charnal house. Early observers were favorable, celebrating the region as "very healthful and delightsome," blessed by a "soveraign Ray of health . . . a serene Air, and a lofty Skie, that defends it from noxious Infection."[23] As early as 1680, however, commentators qualified reports of "generally very healthful" conditions by admitting to "Touches of Auges and fevers" in the summer months. By the mid-1680s the initial optimism had succumbed to Lowcountry realities. Charles Town, in particular, was "extraordinarie sicklie," in "no healthy Scituation . . . and all people that come to the province and Landing there and the most falling sick it brings a Disreputation upon the whole Country."[24] Such reports perhaps discouraged prospective servants.

For another, the colony lacked a large-scale, direct trade with England before the early eighteenth century. Since shipping was irregular and infrequent, passage was difficult to obtain and transport costs high. Further, there was no community of Carolina merchants in England to recruit servants for Lowcountry plantations. Carolina planters were poorly placed to compete for servants against the Chesapeake and the West Indies where major staple trades supported steady shipping and cheap fares and where tobacco and sugar merchants supported a large-scale recruiting network. The effects of these disadvantages are clearly revealed in departure records. Between 1683 and 1686, more than 2,000 indentured servants left Bristol and London for the colonies: only 32 headed for Carolina.[25]

Still, Carolinians had some success in recruiting servants. Headrights records indicate that at least 244 servants were brought to the Lowcountry in the 1670s, 471 in the 1680s (Table 3). In part this success reflects recruiting in Barbados. By 1670, the sugar revolution had produced severe overcrowding and slim prospects for poor men on the island. Servants "out of their time" found their progress blocked. Some took supervisory jobs on large plantations, others worked in Bridgetown, a few became small farmers, but most simply left. During the seventeenth century some 10,000 Barbadians, the majority of them recently freed servants, struck out for other colonies. Some signed new indentures to serve in South Carolina, stark commentary on opportunities on the island. More than a third of the servants in the Lowcountry in the 1670s, perhaps an even higher proportion in the 1680s when depression wracked the sugar industry, arrived by way of Barbados.[26]

Some success, but not enough and not for long. South Carolina's population grew rapidly during the seventeenth century, reaching 4,000 in 1690 and nearly 6,000 by 1700 (Table 1). The small stream of servants from the sugar islands and England failed to keep pace with the number of farms. Further, there were reasons for dissatisfaction with indentured servants. Terms were short, particularly for Barbadians who only had to serve long enough to cover the 50 shilling passage from the island, but also for English servants who could use their options to bargain for better contracts.[27] And they proved difficult to discipline, again particularly the Barbadians, who, perhaps discouraged by their first encounter with American realities, were "soe much addicted to Rum, that they will doe little but whilst the bottle is at their nose."[28] Finally, that small stream was reduced to a mere trickle by the 1690s, inducing the legislature to offer substantial premiums to importers by the decade's end.[29]

Clearly, had Carolinians relied solely on servants they would have faced a labor shortage. Fortunately for the planters (although disastrous for their victims), there were other sources of labor available. One such source, free wage labor, proved even less successful than indentured servitude. South Carolina lived up to its promise as a land of opportunity for poor whites. Planters were able to entice some free workers from Barbados and hire newly freed servants, but high wages and cheap land permitted a quick transition to yeoman status. "'Tis very rare," a Carolina planter explained, "that any freeman will hire himself to labour, after his term of four years are expir'd, by reason they can employ themselves very advantageously in their own business, and on their own land.[30] Fully 85 percent of the servants who appear as free persons in Carolina records eventually became landowners, most of them within a few years of the end of their term.[31]

Indians were another source. While the Indian slave trade was important in South Carolina during the seventeenth century, it only became a major source of labor later, after 1700. Initially, most Indian captives were exported, reflecting perhaps the difficulty of enslaving an indigenous population and the need of Lowcountry planters to earn credits abroad. Some of those Indians were exchanged for West Indian blacks, who soon dominated the Lowcountry work force. Headright claims permit a precise dating of the rise of West Indian blacks and the transition from servants to slaves. Servants outnumbered slaves by more than 7 to 1 in the early 1670s and 4 to 1 from 1675 to 1684, but by only 2 to 1 in the late 1680s. Thereafter, slaves outnumbered servants in headright records, by 1.2 to 1 in the early 1690s and 1.4 to 1 in the middle of the decade (Table 3).[32]

West Indian blacks reached the Lowcountry in two ways. Initially, most arrived as part of the migration from Barbados to South Carolina. Although a majority of those migrants were recently freed servants and poor men without capital, some substantial planters made the move and they brought slaves with them. Sir John Yeamans, for example, brought eight blacks when he arrived from Barbados in June 1671 to assume the colony's governorship.[33] Trade quickly replaced migration as the main source of blacks as Carolinians began shipping livestock, grains, and timber products to Barbados for sugar, bills of exchange, European manufactures, and slaves. Livestock was especially important, as Samuel Wilson explained in 1682: "Hogs increase in Carolina abundantly, and in a manner without any charge or trouble to the Planter. . . . there are many Planters that are single and have never a Servant, that have two or three hundred Hogs, of which they make great profit: Barbados, Jamaica, and New-England, affording a constant good price for their Pork; by

which means they get wherewithal to build them more convenient Houses and to purchase Servants, and Negro-slaves."[34]
Certainly Barbados, with a black population of roughly 50,000 in
1700 and annual deliveries of 2,000 to 4,000 in the last quarter of
the century, had slaves to sell.[35]

One of the most striking things about the transition to slavery
in the Lowcountry is that it occurred at the same time as along
the Tobacco Coast. Simultaneous timing suggests similarity in
process. In the Chesapeake colonies the transition emerged out
of a complex set of changes in the supply and demand for labor.
Before 1680, the great majority of unfree workers in Maryland
and Virginia were indentured servants who were not sharply
distinguished from the planters they served and who could expect to become masters in their own right. As the century pro-
gressed, however, planters found it increasingly difficult to obtain
enough such workers to meet their need for labor. A declining
population and slowly rising real wages in England created improved opportunities at home, while the opening up of Pennsylvania, the beginnings of rapid development in the Carolinas, and
continued growth along the tobacco coast and in the sugar islands
led to greater colonial competition for workers. The result was a
labor shortage in the Chesapeake and a change in the composition of the work force as planters purchased slaves to replace
servants. In Maryland, for example, servants outnumbered slaves
by nearly 4 to 1 in estate inventories probated in the late 1670s; in
the early 1690s, there were nearly four slaves for every servant.[36]

While it is unlikely that planters in the Chesapeake or the
Lowcountry understood the larger processes behind these shifts,
the price signals they received were clear (Table 4). Servant
prices moved sharply upward during the period of transition,
rising by 50 percent from 1675 to 1690. Slave prices, by contrast,
were fairly stable in the last third of the seventeenth century,
although they did jump up around 1700. As a result, the prices of
the two types of workers converged. In the mid-1670s, slaves cost

Chesapeake planters nearly three times the price of a servant. In 1690, they were less than twice as expensive. Slaves had become a better buy.

The first transition to slavery in the Lowcountry resembled the process along the tobacco coast in still another way: it was not the product of a major change in the agricultural base of the regional economy. Some historians have asserted the contrary, contending that the Lowcountry transition resembled that of Barbados. There, a shift from an agriculture based on tobacco, cotton, and food crops grown on small farms to sugar produced on large plantations triggered the move toward slavery. The Barbadian sugar revolution raised demand for labor beyond the capacity of the servant trade and created conditions of work and opportunities that were not attractive to British youths. The spread of rice culture did have such consequences in Carolina during the early decades of the eighteenth century. However, the Lowcountry became a slave society before it developed a plantation regime, when small farms still dominated production, and while agriculture remained focused on food crops, livestock, and timber for the West Indian market.[37]

While the transition to slavery in both the Chesapeake and the Lowcountry was triggered by a decline in the supply of servants and a rise in their price, there was one major difference in the process. Both regions relied heavily on the sugar islands for slaves during the seventeenth century, but Chesapeake planters were able to call on shipments directly from Africa as early as the mid-1670s, perhaps thirty years before Carolinians were able to do so.[38] That difference probably reflects the larger market in the Chesapeake and the greater wealth of tobacco planters. Lowcountry planters offered a steady market for small shipments of West Indian blacks and they could pay for them with products much in demand on the sugar islands. However, they would have had trouble absorbing the much larger cargoes typically handled by African slavers, they lacked exports that merchants would accept in exchange for blacks, and few of them were rich enough to command credit in England. In the seventeenth century, the Lowcountry was simply not an attractive market for African slave traders.

The Second Transition: Toward African Slavery

The conditions that denied Lowcountry planters direct access to the African slave trade disappeared after 1700. While it is not certain when direct trade began, it is clear that slave imports grew dramatically during the early decades of the eighteenth century. On average, Charles Town merchants imported 275 blacks a year during the 1710s, nearly 900 in the 1720s, and over 2,000 in the 1730s (Table 5). Those figures, furthermore, understate the actual volume, particularly during the 1710s. Given the population sizes reported in Table 1, these import data imply a rate of natural increase of more than 5 percent annually from 1710 to 1720, a most unlikely if not impossible pace. If we assume that birth and death rates in the slave population were equal, imports must have been twice as high, 550 per year. In any case, the direct trade with Africa had become a major supplier of Lowcountry workers by the second decade of the eighteenth century.[39]

The growth of the Lowcountry rice industry was a key event in that process. During the seventeenth century, South Carolinians engaged in a systematic search for an agricultural staple that would command a direct European market. They tried a variety of crops, testing both the local resource base and overseas demand. The period of experimentation ended successfully in the 1690s with the commercial cultivation of rice, the crop that "soon became the chief support of the colony, and its great source of opulence," "as much their staple Commodity, as Sugar is to Barbados and Jamaica, or Tobacco to Virginia and Maryland."[40] The beginnings of commercial rice cultivation in the Lowcountry are obscure and the subject of some controversy, but data on exports are available from 1699, shortly after the start of successful production. These describe a very rapid expansion during the first three decades of the eighteenth century: rice exports passed 1.5 million pounds by 1710, 6 million in 1720, and nearly 20 million in 1730.[41]

Most historians have attributed the beginnings of a direct slave trade with Africa and the rapid growth of the Lowcountry slave population to the expansion of rice culture. Clarence Ver Steeg has questioned that link, suggesting instead that naval stores played the key role. The production of naval stores gave the economy of South Carolina a major boost early in the eighteenth century, although in the long run they proved far less important than rice. The English government, reacting to wartime disruption of its supply from the Baltic, provided the incentive for the industry in 1705 in the form of bounties for tar, pitch, resin, turpentine, hemp, masts, yards, and bowsprits produced in the colonies. The incentives worked and the South Carolina naval stores industry grew rapidly. Charleston exports of pitch and tar exceeded 6,500 barrels in 1712, 50,000 in 1718, and peaked at nearly 60,000 in 1725 before falling off in sharp decline.[42]

Ver Steeg asserts that there was little relationship between the expansion of rice and slave imports during the first quarter of the eighteenth century but that there was a strong relationship between the production of naval stores and the arrival of blacks, a "statistical correlation . . . corroborated by contemporary observers." While it is clear that slave imports grew rapidly after Parliament established the bounty system, Ver Steeg's argument is difficult to evaluate. The data on slave imports (Table 5) are inconsistent and understate the true volume of the trade. Further, data on exports, particularly naval stores, are spotty. Nevertheless, there is a strong relationship between slave imports and exports of pitch and tar. However, slave imports show an equally strong relationship to rice exports and an even stronger relationship to all exports. Apparently, the rapid Africanization of South Carolina in the early eighteenth century was not a function of the growth of rice production or the rise of the naval stores industry, but of both, or, more precisely, of the general expansion of Lowcountry exports.[43]

The evidence that the rapid growth of slavery in the early

eighteenth century reflected a general expansion of exports rather than the rise of a particular product is supported by *post-mortem* inventories. During the first third of the century many great planters ran diverse operations, producing rice, naval stores, corn, peas, beef, and pork for export to England and the West Indies. Francis Courage, for example, used 16 slaves to grow rice and corn, make pitch, and tend substantial herds of cattle, sheep, and horses in the mid-1720s.[44] Often they combined agriculture and trade to participate in all aspects of the Lowcountry economy. The Charles Town merchant Francis Holmes, for example, traded to Barbados, Jamaica, and Boston, exchanging provisions for rum, sugar, and slaves in his own small sloop, kept a store stocked with dry goods, groceries, and tools, worked the deerskin and rice trades, and loaned money in the local mortgage market. He also ran a plantation at James Island where his 15 slaves grew rice and tended livestock.[45]

These diverse operations provide a clue to one of the mysteries surrounding the growth of slavery, how it was financed. The Africanization of the Carolina Lowcountry was expensive. The roughly 9000 slaves imported during the 1720s cost perhaps £180,000 sterling, more than £100 for each white householder in the colony. Some of the capital was supplied by West Indian planters, some by English merchants and lawyers, but most was generated locally. Planters were able to borrow funds to finance expansion in the local credit market, where Charles Town merchants loaned money earned in the provisions and Indian trade on mortgages secured by land and, especially, slaves.[46]

By and large, the planters were good risks, for two reasons. Many had, in the first place, accumulated small estates through the process of farm building, slowly clearing land, erecting barns, fencing, and houses, planting orchards, and raising livestock herds. Once planters had "established their characters for honesty and industry" and built up some capital that could be used to secure loans, they could obtain credit and purchase "negroes to assist them," thus financing a subsequent and more rapid expansion.[47] Secondly, the diverse export sector provided a variety of work opportunities for slaves and produced handsome returns for their masters. Table 6 describes income from crops and naval stores on 27 estates probated in the Lowcountry between 1716 and 1731. The slaves on those plantations produced an annual income of 20 percent of their appraised value from such products alone. Clearly, Lowcountry planters were good risks.

A rapidly expanding export sector, handsome profits, and substantial slave imports suggest a dramatic increase in demand for labor, the key element in accounting for the changing composition of the Lowcountry work force. The prospect of high returns and great wealth set Carolinians off on a vicious scramble for workers, led them to take great risks not only with their estates but with the colony's survival, and produced a thorough transformation of Lowcountry society that proved destructive and oppressive to its victims, frightening and unsettling to its masters. The transformation was hardly tidy and it was purchased at great cost by a sometimes savage brutality, but we can make some progress toward understanding the process by examining the several constituent groups who labored on Lowcountry plantations: whites, particularly indentured servants, Native Americans, slaves from the West Indies, and African blacks.

Servants played little role in the Lowcountry economy after the 1680s. They were only 2 percent of the unfree workers in 1708, and only a handful appear in probate inventories taken between 1690 and 1730 (Table 7). Carolina planters faced the declining supply of servants that afflicted all of British America, but conditions specific to the Lowcountry aggravated the shortage. In the first place, Carolina planters had relied heavily on a secondary market in servants who completed their terms in Barbados, a supply that dried up as white migration to the island dwindled.[48] Secondly, the growth of the export sector made the Lowcountry a less attractive destination for poor British youths. Plantation agriculture brought with it a black majority, gang labor, higher mortality, and diminished opportunities. Rice cultivation in particular was unpleasant, to put it mildly, a "horrible employment not far short of digging in Potosi."[49]

It is also possible that Africanization and the rise of plantation agriculture reshaped planter preferences, persuaded them that blacks were better workers than whites, or at least better suited to the work of the Lowcountry. By the Revolutionary era the belief that the region "was not capable of being cultivated by white men" was central to the ideology of the great planters.[50] "White servants would have exhausted their strength in clearing a spot of land for digging their own graves, and every rice plantation would have served no other purpose than a burying ground to its European cultivators," Alexander Hewatt explained. "The low lands of Carolina . . . must have long remained a wilderness, had not Africans, whose natural constitutions were suited to the climate and work, been employed in cultivating this useful article of food and commerce." However, such attitudes appear only after the Lowcountry had become a thoroughly Africanized slave society, receiving clear expression for the first time around 1740 during the debate over the introduction of slavery in Georgia.[51] It is unlikely that planter preferences played a major role in the decline of indentured servitude in the Lowcountry. Planters took what servants they could get. Supply—the preferences of potential servants and the availability of slaves—was the critical variable.

This is not to imply that planter attitudes played no role in the growth of slavery. Attitudes were essential, in at least two ways. First, planters had to be willing to substitute slaves for servants, to treat blacks differently than whites, to subject slaves to a harsh, degrading and severe discipline. Second, planters had to be persuaded that blacks could be employed profitably, turned with success to the tasks at hand. In both the West Indian origins of so many Lowcountry whites was crucial, for the experience of the sugar islands had shaped racial attitudes and demonstrated that black slaves could be used to exploit a range of opportunities.[52] Attitudes acquired in the Caribbean may explain why white Carolinians turned to slavery so quickly, without hesitation, and with such apparent enthusiasm. Attitudes cannot account for the timing of changes in the composition of the work force, however:

that can be understood only by close attention to markets, to the supply of workers from various sources and the demand for labor.

While the rapid disappearance of servants from field work is simple enough to account for, their failure to dominate plantation crafts and supervisory positions early in the Africanization process is a puzzle. In the West Indies and the Chesapeake colonies the transition from servitude to slavery occurred in two phases: blacks first displaced whites in routine agricultural labor and only later, with the rise of an acculturated, country-born slave population, dominated skilled work and supervision.[53] Peter Wood argues that a more complex pattern prevailed in the Lowcountry as blacks captured, lost, and then recaptured a dominant position in skilled jobs.[54] The evidence from probate inventories does not support Wood's contention: none of the slave men who appear in inventories probated before 1720 were described as skilled, but 7 percent of those who appear in the 1720s and 10 percent in the 1730s were so described, a pattern similar to that found elsewhere in British America in the early stages of the rise of slavery.[55] What distinguishes Carolina from the other British colonies is the failure of Lowcountry planters to import white servants to perform such tasks before a substantial number of skilled blacks appeared in the region.

Another distinguishing feature of the Lowcountry labor system during the process of Africanization was the key role played by Native American slaves. While Indian slaves appear in South Carolina as early as 1683, they were rare during the seventeenth century. In 1700 there were roughly 200 enslaved Indians in the Lowcountry, 3 percent of the total population and 7 percent of the unfree work force. During the next decade they were the most rapidly growing group in the colony. By 1710 there were 1500 Native American slaves accounting for 15 percent of the total and 26 percent of the bound laborers. They continued to increase in the next decade, but much less rapidly. In 1720, there were 2000 Indians, but they made up only 11 percent of the total and 17 percent of the slaves. Thereafter both their numbers and their share fell sharply: in 1730 there were 500 Indian slaves in South Carolina, less than 2 percent of the total and only 2.4 percent of the unfree workers (Table 1).

While the subject merits a detailed investigation, the pattern is consistent with an explanation based on the supply of Indians and the demand for labor. During the seventeenth century before the rapid expansion of the Carolina export sector, Lowcountry planters met their labor needs with servants and West Indian blacks. Few Indians were turned into slaves and most of them were exported to earn foreign exchange. In this period the slave trade was a secondary activity, subordinate to the trade in deer skins and the political aims of the English and their Native American allies. Indian slaves were captured almost incidentally, as a by-product of other processes. After 1700 the Lowcountry export boom led to a sharp increase in demand for labor which transformed relationships between the English and the Indians. The slave trade gained in importance and was no longer subordinated to the deerskin trade or to political concerns. More Indians were captured and more of those captives were kept in the Lowcountry to make rice, grow provisions, and produce naval stores.[56]

The intensification of the slave trade proved devastating to the aboriginal population. It was a bloody, violent business, impossible to institutionalize, that demanded increased warfare and ever more raiding. It produced sharp demographic decline and the total destruction of several smaller tribes. And it led to major political changes as Indians struggled to protect themselves by forming larger and more effective federations and by elaborating a "play-off" system in which rivalries between the English, French, and Spanish were exploited in efforts to control the worst excesses of the European invasion. Population decline and political restructuring quickly lowered the supply of Indian slaves, reducing it to a mere trickle by the 1720s.[57]

It is unlikely that planter preferences for Africans played a major role in the decline of Indian slavery. True, Indians were more vulnerable to Lowcountry diseases than blacks and were thus more often sick and more likely to die young. Indians also may have found escape easier given their geographic knowledge and the presence of nearby tribes who might take them in. And it is possible that tradition and prior work experience made Indians less productive as agricultural laborers. However, such differences were compensated for by the higher prices blacks commanded: during the 1720s adult blacks were worth 40 to 50 percent more than adult Indians. If planter preferences were responsible for the decline of Indian slavery one would expect a sharp fall in price to accompany the fall in numbers. Prices rose, rather than fell, by 50 to 100 percent from the 1720s to 1730s, indicating that planters would have purchased more Indian slaves had they been available.[58]

Although the preferences of planters as individual managers of labor played little role in the decline of Indian slavery, their political concerns, the preferences of planters as a collective, as members of an emerging ruling class, were critical to the fall of the native slave trade. In the late stages of the Yamasee War the Carolina Assembly passed an Indian Trading Act which, among other things, restricted dealing in Native American slaves. Perhaps that reflected the tension between the extravagant violence of the slave trade and the growing gentility of Lowcountry life, a tension that Bernard Bailyn has identified as a central theme of colonial history.[59] More likely it was a reaction to the dangers posed by the Indian slave trade. Those dangers were clearly revealed in the Yamasee War, which engulfed the colony in 1715–1717. While the origins of that conflict are complex, it is clear that Indian grievances against the slave trade helped initiate it and that the slave traders welcomed it as an opportunity to increase supplies and prevented an early settlement. The war devasted the colony: some 400 people were killed, more than £100,000 in property was lost, half the cultivated land was abandoned, food supplies were so short that starvation threatened, commerce was disrupted, and taxes rose sharply. And it was nearly worse. Only luck and skillful diplomacy prevented the alliance of Creeks, Choctaws, and Yamasees from overwhelming Carolina and pushing the settlers into the sea. By 1715, the Carolina planters had too much at stake to tolerate such risks, especially since an alternative (and safer) source of labor was available through the African trade.[60]

The rapid growth of the slave trade to the West Indies during the seventeenth century, long before Africans emerged as a dominant source of unfree labor in the Lowcountry, played a central role in the rise of slavery in South Carolina and in all the other mainland colonies. In only two decades around 1650, Barbados was transformed from a struggling tobacco colony into a major sugar producer. By 1660 there were 34,000 blacks in the British West Indies and annual slave deliveries approached 3,000. The transformation is usually credited to the Dutch, who, "being ingaged on the coast of Giney in Affrick for negros slaves having lost Brasille not knowing where to vent them they trusted them to Barbados." The English played at least a minor role in this early West Indian slave trade and, by the 1660s, had wrested the African trade (as well as all the other major trades with its colonies) from Dutch control.[61] During the third quarter of the seventeenth century, English slavers greatly improved the efficiency of their operations. Prices fell dramatically, reaching a low point in the 1680s. At the same time, volume rose sharply: in the 1680s the Royal African Company delivered more than 5,000 slaves annually to the British sugar islands, a figure that excludes the apparently substantial trade conducted by interlopers.[62] The supply of slaves to British America improved during the seventeenth century, the larger numbers and lower prices reflecting more efficient markets, cheaper transport costs, and the exploitation of new African sources. At the very least the long-run supply curve for slaves was highly elastic, and despite rising prices evident by the 1690s, it remained so into the early decades of the eighteenth century.

These developments proved critical to mainland planters. For one thing, the large slave population of the islands provided a source of labor, one easily integrated into the provisions trades between the continent and the West Indies. Further, mainland planters found themselves in the fortunate position of a minor market for a rapidly expanding supply of workers. Once they were willing to pay the price, Carolina planters would be able to get all the slaves they needed.

As we have seen, Carolina planters relied on the West Indies for slaves from the start of settlement in the Lowcountry. While demand remained low, that reliance posed few problems. West Indian markets were easily able to supply the 100 to 200 slaves a year that Carolina planters could afford before 1710. Indeed, at those levels it was probably cheaper to acquire slaves that way than through the direct trade with Africa. Lowcountry planters could take advantage of the large and efficient island slave markets; transactions were easily integrated into the provisions trade; and blacks could be purchased in small lots without driving up their price. However, the rapid growth of demand for labor fueled by the export boom soon stretched the capacity of this secondary trade. When the Lowcountry proved capable of absorbing 500 to 1,000 and more slaves each year, certainly the case by the 1720s if not earlier, the relative advantages of the island slave trade diminished and the direct trade in Africans emerged as the chief source of workers for Carolina plantations.

Although safer than dealing in Indian slaves, the Africanization of the Lowcountry work force was not without risks. Some of those risks were private, faced by planters as individuals. Many planters responded too robustly to the export boom, overextended themselves in purchasing slaves to cash in on the opportunities, and went under in the short-term downswings that punctuated the secular expansion. There were also public risks in creating a slave society with a substantial black majority, risks that led to a gnawing fear of internal enemies, fear that reached a fever pitch whenever signs (real or imagined) of insurrection appeared. In attempting to control those risks, the great planters of the

Caroline Lowcountry took the first halting steps in the slow process of becoming a regional ruling class.[63]

Conclusion

By 1730 the central features of the Lowcountry plantation regime were firmly established. It was clearly a slave society, its 20,000 blacks, many of them newly arrived Africans, a substantial majority of the population. Those blacks were both heavily concentrated in the hands of a few great planters and widely distributed among white householders. More than 80 percent of the estates probated in 1730 reported slaves and a quarter of them possessed at least 20 blacks (Table 7). In addition, the region was very prosperous, its lively export sector focused on rice production capable of supporting an impressive growth rate. It remained only for the great planters to consolidate their power, to develop the sense of group consciousness, and to forge the ideology that would transform them into an effective ruling class.

The structure of the Atlantic labor market played a key role in shaping that regime. The developers of the Lowcountry had several options in recruiting and organizing a work force. They could draw on free workers and indentured servants from Britain and the sugar islands, on Indian slaves from the vast North American interior, and on blacks from the West Indies and Africa. With the exception of African slaves, those workers moved in small, localized markets characterized by sharp, unpredictable shifts in volume and price. Africans, by contrast, were trapped in a much wider net, commodities in a stable, large-scale, international labor market that made them the victims of choice in the rapidly expanding plantation colonies of European America.

TABLE 1   Estimated Population of South Carolina, 1670–1750

	Whites	Blacks	Indian Slaves	Total
1670	170	30		200
1680	1,000	200		1,200
1690	2,400	1,500	100	3,900
1700	3,300	2,400	200	5,900
1710	4,200	4,300	1,500	10,000
1720	6,500	9,900	2,000	18,400
1730	10,000	20,000	500	30,500
1740	15,000	36,700		51,700
1750	25,000	39,000		64,000

SOURCES: U.S. Bureau of the Census, *Historical Statistics of the United States, Colonial Times to 1970* (Washington, D.C., Government Printing Office, 1975), series Z16, p. 1168; Peter H. Wood, *Black Majority: Negroes in Colonial South Carolina from 1670 through the Stono Rebellion* (New York, Alfred A. Knopf, 1975), pp. 146–147, 153n, 155; William Robert Snell, "Indian Slavery in Colonial South Carolina, 1671–1795," Ph.D. Dissertation, University of Alabama, 1972, p. 96; and below, Table 7.

TABLE 2   The South Carolina Population in 1703 and 1708.

	1703	1708
free men	1,460	1,360
free women	940	900
free children	1,200	1,700
White servant men	110	60
White servant women	90	60
Total Whites	3,800	4,080
Negro men slaves	1,500	1,800
Negro women slaves	900	1,100
Negro children slaves	600	1,200
Total Negros	3,000	4,100
Indian Men slaves	100	500
Indian woman slaves	150	600
Indian children slaves	100	300
Total Indian Slaves	350	1,400
Total	7,150	9,580

SOURCE: Governor and Council of Carolina to the Council of Trade and Plantations, Carolina, 17 Sept. 1709, CO 5/1264, 82.

TABLE 3   Servant, Free, and Slave Migrants to South Carolina,
           1670–1696

	Servants	Free	White	Black	Servants/Blacks
1670–74	188	186	374	25	7.52
1675–79	56	70	126	14	4.00
1680–84	374	221	595	91	4.12
1685–89	97	54	151	45	2.16
1690–94	33	23	56	38	0.85
1695–96	45	87	132	62	0.73
Total	793	641	1434	276	2.87

SOURCE: Alexander S. Salley, ed., *Warrants for Land in South Carolina (1672–1711)*, 3 vols. (Columbia, S.C., Historical Commission of South Carolina, 1910–15).

TABLE 4   Prices of Servants and Slaves in British America,
1675–1702

	Maryland Servants	Maryland Slaves	British Amer. Slaves	Barbadian Slaves
1675	L8.0	L23.0	L21.92	L15.04
1676				14.22
1677				16.80
1678	9.0	23.5		13.50
1679				18.59
1680			19.32	13.01
1681	11.0	25.5		13.21
1682				14.08
1683				12.41
1684	10.5	23.0		12.78
1685			19.95	
1686				13.28
1687	11.5	23.0		12.42
1688				13.15
1689				14.17
1690	12.0	22.0	23.85	16.27
1691				14.29
1692				14.49
1693	10.0	24.5		16.22
1694				16.94
1695			26.02	20.44
1696	10.5	25.5		23.16
1697				17.48
1698				15.80
1699	11.5	26.5		15.19
1700			23.68	24.71
1701				20.21
1702	12.0	28.0		21.77

Notes and Sources: Maryland servants: Prices are three-year averages for males with four or more years to serve, in Maryland currency. Russell R. Menard, "From Servants to Slaves: The Transformation of the Chesapeake Labor System," *Southern Studies,* 16 (1977), p. 372.

Maryland slaves: Prices are three-year averages for male field hands aged 16 to 32, in Maryland currency. *Ibid.*

British American Slaves. Prices are five year averages in sterling. U.S. Bureau of the Census, *Historical Statistics of the United States, Colonial Times to 1970* (Washington, D.C., Government Printing Office, 1975), 1174, Ser. Z 166.

Barbadian Slaves: Prices are weighted averages of men, women, and children sold at auction by the Royal African Company in sterling. David W. Galenson, *Traders, Planters, and Slaves: Market Behavior in Early English America* (Cambridge, Cambridge University Press, 1986), p. 65.

TABLE 5   CHARLES TOWN SLAVE IMPORTS, 1706–1740

Year	Slaves	Year	Slaves
1706	24	1724	800
1707	22	1725	439
1708	53	1726	1751
1709	107	1727	1794
1710	131	1728	1201
1711	170	1729	1499
1712	76	1730	941
1713	159	1731	1766
1714	419	1732	1199
1715	81	1733	2792
1716	67	1734	1805
1717	619	1735	2907
1718	566	1736	3526
1719	541	1737	2246
1720	601	1738	2508
1721	1739	1739	2017
1722	323	1740	740
1723	463	Total	34518

SOURCES: Peter H. Wood, *Black Majority: Negores in Colonial South Carolina from 1670 through the Stono Rebellion* (New York, Alfred A. Knopf, 1974), p. 151; U.S. Bureau of the Census, *Historical Statistics of the United States, Colonial Times to 1970* (Washington, D.C., Government Printing Office, 1975), series Z 155, p. 1173. For 16 of the years, Wood and W. Robert Higgins (who compiled the series for *Historical Statistics*) reported different figures. In each case I used the higher number, reflecting my sense that these data understate the true volume of slave imports. Using the lower figure in each instance of disagreement yields a total of 27,115.

TABLE 6   Earnings from Crops Reported in Probate Inventories, 1716–1731

Category	# Estates	Value of Slaves	Value of Crops	% Earned
<10%	5	7455	508	7%
10–19%	9	31030	4241	14%
20–29%	8	26693	6316	24%
30 + %	5	16215	5327	33%
Total	27	81393	16392	20%

SOURCES: Records of the Secretary of the Province, 1711–1719, 1714–1717, 1721–1722, 1722–1726; Wills, Inventories & Miscellaneous Records, 1722–1724, 1724–1725, 1729–1731, South Carolina Department of Archives and History.

TABLE 7   Unfree Workers in Carolina Probate Inventories, 1678–1730.

	1678–90	1691–1700	1711–18	1721–24	1730
# Estates	22	29	8	121	29
# with labor	12	19	5	93	24
# Servants	9	0	1	3	3
# Blacks	36	73	47	1303	456
# Indians & Mustees	5	5	6	88	12
Total Workers	50	78	54	1394	471
Workers/ Estates	2.3	2.7	6.8	11.5	16.2
Estates with 10–19 workers	2	3	3	9	3
20–49 workers	0	0	0	15	6
50–99 workers	0	0	0	6	2
100 + workers	0	0	0	1	0

SOURCES: Records of the Secretary of the Province, 1675–1695, 1692–1700, 1700–1710, 1711–1719, 1714–1717, 1721–1722, 1722–1726; Wills, Inventories & Miscellaneous Records, 1722–1724, 1724–1725, 1729–1731, South Carolina Department of Archives and History.

Talking with Indians:
Interpreters and Diplomacy
in French Louisiana

PATRICIA GALLOWAY

If there was one lasting effect of the Indian policy of Pierre Le
Moyne d'Iberville, founder of the Louisiana colony, it was the
establishment of a corps of interpreters skilled in the Indian
languages of the Old Southwest. These interpreters, consciously
given over by the leaders of the colony to native culture and its
values, were instrumental in maintaining French hegemony in
Louisiana in spite of low population, trade goods shortages, and
English pressure.

The French experience in Canada had shown that knowledge
of the native languages was vital if the twin goals of conversion
and economic exploitation were to be greeted with any coopera-
tion at all by the Indians. As early as Cartier's third voyage in
1541, young French boys were left among the Indians to learn
their language, and this policy was successfully continued by
Champlain in 1610–1611, founding the Canadian corps of interpreters on several young men sent among the Hurons and Algon-
quins.[1] These first young men were the beginning of the famed
voyageurs and *coureurs de bois* who carried the commerce in furs
into the backwoods, and from this earliest beginning they exhibited the tendency to acculturate to the host Indian society that
was to mark French interpreters throughout the history of
French colonialism in North America.

A tolerance and understanding of the necessity for some limited acculturation by Europeans sprang from the general French
attitude toward the Indian, which was certainly as exploitative as
that of any other Europeans, but was noticeably less racist.[2] For
some time, and particularly in Canada, official policy condoned

and even encouraged marriages between Frenchmen and Christianized Indian women, with the acknowledged goal of eventual amalgamation of the two populations.[3]

To understand Indian policy in Louisiana, one should remember that Iberville and his brothers, who among them more or less controlled Indian policy in the Louisiana colony for some forty of its sixty years of existence, were Canadians themselves, and so were many of the early settlers they brought with them. Hence it was Canadian attitudes that strongly influenced their official behavior toward the Indians. It was from the Canadian experience that Iberville's proposed pacification policy arose. His intention was to cause the different Indian nations to move into settlements where they would be convenient to French evangelizing and economic exploitation. He did not take account of the fact that where many of the Canadian Indians were hunter-gatherers whose minimally fixed abodes made the efforts of missionaries nearly impossible, the southeastern Indians were mostly sedentary farmers who would not have to be followed around all year.

Iberville further intended to bring warring Indians together under the peacemaking aegis of France, but this policy ignored the fact that European competition for Indian markets and alliances was already forcing a corresponding Indian competition that could not be easily solved. By the time he arrived on the Gulf coast, English colonials had already begun arming tribes of the interior with the purpose of making them into slave-catchers of other tribes; Iberville's brother Bienville would earn the lasting gratitude of the Choctaw not for having made peace, but for having armed them against the slaving depredations of the English-backed Chickasaws and Creeks. Yet however flawed were these initial plans, they were soon altered by realities on the ground. This healthy dose of *Realpolitik* came from the beginnings of understanding of the Indians and their aspirations, fostered early by both Iberville's interpreter policy and his brother Bienville's own facility with native languages.

Canadian missionaries had discovered that learning American Indian languages was not necessarily easy: "Those who know what languages are will rightly consider that to learn one without books and almost without an interpreter, among wandering people, and in the midst of several other occupations, is not the work of a day."[4] But the young men Cartier and Champlain had chosen had not had such problems, and the cabin boys who were Iberville's first choice for interpreter candidates were likewise much better equipped by their youth to learn a language "without books." Besides, the tribes of the Old Southwest did not wander, and the boys had no other occupation to distract them, at least not while they were learning the languages.

The boys initially chosen for Louisiana were all military enlistees, and though it is hard for us to imagine anything but childish conduct from boys of eight or ten, in the early eighteenth century childhood was considered to have ended by that time,[5] and these boys had already been subject to military discipline for some time before they were chosen for the task. Among the Indians they would not only acquire a deep knowledge of the language, but also of the culture of their hosts, for although they were entering the tribe at an age that was too great for them to join the youngest boys, they were doubtless put in the charge of old men and given the same course of instruction as other young men qualifying for manhood. And because they were boys whose European acculturation was not yet complete—who had been placed as cabin-boys as a form of apprenticeship for adult life[6]— inevitably their European acculturation was not completed; instead, cut off from European contact and completing their education among the Indians, they adopted many of the ideals and attitudes of their teachers.

The Canadian experience had taught the French the efficacy of such acculturation of their interpreters, since it proved so valuable in the conduct of diplomacy. Interpreters thus trained in the Indian culture would understand, in a way no anthropologist ever could, what the Indian culture meant by war and peace, alliance and enmity: the fine gradations of those categories and the borderline cases. The price would be that with understanding came sympathy and allegiance, but the French had learned that the advantages made such a price affordable.

The reason for choosing cadets and cabin boys rather than younger children as interpreter candidates was the value that literacy added to the service they could perform. Although these young men would certainly not be linguistic stylists in their mother tongue, they would have had a modicum of schooling.[7] This was an indispensable requirement, for part of their work included the transcription of diplomatic transactions to become part of the permanent record of meetings and agreements with the Indians.[8] Literacy was also indispensable if the interpreters were to make reports of the intelligence-gathering they were expected to do.[9] Part of the job was to gauge the mood and intentions of Indian leaders, villages, and tribes as a whole, and their reports were used in the formation of strategic policy.

The significance of both roles of the interpreters can hardly be overestimated, for if the importance of Indian goodwill to the survival of Canada had been inarguable, such was far more the case for Louisiana. Never given adequate support from the home country, farmed out to one financier after another in an effort to increase settlement, the Louisiana colony suffered from a chronic lack of French population.[10] By contrast, the English colonies of the eastern seaboard teemed with people and exerted from the start a westward pressure that threatened the French colony. It was clear to the colony's founders—and it remained clear toward the end of its history—that the favor and active support of the Indian tribes of the interior was a condition of the colony's existence.[11] From its very earliest days the colony faced an open threat from its English neighbors to the east, who claimed the lands of the interior at least as far as the Mississippi River. They were in the process of making good on that claim and thwarting La Salle's thrust to the Gulf via the Mississippi when parried by the French initiative under Iberville. The instrument of this English push to the interior was trade with the Indians in deerskins and Indian slaves.

The first European landing on an American shore made it inevitable that the Indians of the continent would be drawn into the developing capitalist world-economy as "underdeveloped" suppliers of raw materials and consumers of manufactured goods.[12] In the southeast the English were the most aggressive force in this drive. It was no accident that this was the case; active prosecution of the Indian trade had been a part of English imperial policy in the southern colonies from the beginning.[13] Indian traders sent into the interior enjoyed governmental subsidy and Indian trade was used as the entering wedge for the militarization of the frontier region.

But for a time the most prized raw material of the interior was the Indian slave taken by other Indians armed with guns through alliance with the English.[14] This activity had already begun to affect the tribes of the deep interior as far as the Mississippi by the end of the seventeenth century, and it was a primary factor in the willingness of the Choctaw to attempt to redress the balance by allying themselves with the French colonists.[15] It was the Indian notion of alliance, which included fictive adoption of members of the allied group, that fitted so well with the French idea of interpreter training.

To understand the real contribution of the interpreters to French colonial policy, the fairly circumscribed example of eastern Louisiana makes a useful set piece. The colony endured for only sixty-four years and the interpreters in that part of it had to do with only one major language family. The activities of Indian diplomacy were concentrated on Mobile and its two dependent posts, Fort Toulouse on the Alabama River from 1716 and Fort Tombecbé on the Tombigbee from 1736.

The first Louisiana interpreters were Iberville's "cabin boys." The personnel lists for the expeditions of 1699 and 1700 show six cabin boys each, some of them the same:

1699	*1700*
St. Michel	St. Michel
Gabriel Marcal	Gabriel Martial
Jean Joly	Jean Joly
Jacques Charon	Jacques Charron
Pierre Huet	Francois Moreau
Pierre LeVasseur	Jacques Dupont[16]

Iberville did send cabin boys among the Indians, and they were probably some or all of these, but it is harder to establish with certainty who they were and what their specific backgrounds may have been.[17]

We do know at least part of the story of one of the boys, as his story was bound up with the first French effort to weld a Choctaw-Chickasaw alliance against the English. The young cabin-boy St. Michel, son of the captain of the port at La Rochelle,[18] was with Iberville on the first voyage and was left behind with the infant colony. According to Iberville, he had used the opportunity to learn the Choctaw-like language of the Houma tribe located on the lower Mississippi. In 1702, at the end of a meeting with Choctaw and Chickasaw representatives designed to stop the English-sponsored slave-raiding by the Chickasaw on the Choctaw, and at the request of the Chickasaw, Iberville sent St. Michel to live with them and learn their language.[19] A year later, as the officer Boisbriant met in the Choctaw villages with Choctaws and Chickasaws, again to negotiate alliances, the Choctaw alleged that the Chickasaw had murdered the boy, and when Chickasaw emissaries failed to return with him, Boisbriant turned the Chickasaw representatives over to the Choctaw for revenge for prior wrongs. But St. Michel had not been killed, as the Chickasaws said, for they brought him back at the end of the year.[20]

The stories of others of the cabin boys are not so clear. Iberville says that in 1700 he sent another of them to the Natchez to learn their language.[21] Pénicaut adds that a boy had been left with a Bayougoula chief in 1700, that in the space of a few weeks he had acquired the ability to converse, and that Iberville had left him there to serve as an interpreter "for the French who should pass this way."[22] Probably all of the cabin boys of the 1700 list were so employed, but as yet no clear connection can be made between the names of these boys that we know and those of the later interpreters.[23]

A garrison list of 1702 indicates that there were twelve of these cabin boys assigned to the garrison of the Mobile post for the purpose of learning languages,[24] although they would actually have lived among the tribes. This policy of fostering young cabin-boys and cadets among the Indian nations remained in force not just in the early days but throughout the history of the colony. In 1708 Nicolas de la Salle's census listed six cabin-boys "both to learn the Indian languages and to serve at sea and assist the workmen on land,"[25] and that same year Bienville wrote that he had sent one to the Choctaw and another to the Chickasaw.[26] The Minister of Colonies in France, Pontchartrain, not only approved of this measure but advised that "it is necessary to have some likewise among the neighboring nations whose languages are unknown to the French."[27] Later Ministers favored the same policy. After the return of the colony from private monopoly to the crown in 1732, Maurepas wrote directing Bienville to "choose from the number of young cadets who are serving in this government those whom he thinks most intelligent in order to learn the Indian languages so that they may be able some day to serve as interpreters and to win the confidence of the Indians."[28] The same year the officer Louboey, at that time serving in New Orleans, urged the minister to have the eleven-year-old boy Massé, orphaned in the Natchez revolt of 1729, accepted as a cadet because he had "a very good aptitude for the Mobile language. . ."[29] As late as 1745, Louisiana governor Vaudreuil was still assigning young cadets to learn Indian languages.[30]

This picture of cabin boys and cadets maturing into the job is, however, an idealized one, for several of the interpreters were adults of Canadian origin, just like the Le Moynes. Conditions during the colony's early years, when poor or completely failed crops compelled the governor to send his men to live among the Indians, inevitably supplied the opportunity for maturer men with apititude and motivation to learn the languages of their hosts.

Beinville himself served as a model for young officers of ambition. He wrote retrospectively in a 1726 memoir: "Confined as I was in an unknown world with such a small troop I applied myself first to putting myself in a position to govern by myself and without the aid of an interpreter in the language that appeared to me to be the most predominant among the Indians and the knowledge of which could make the others easy for me in the future."[31] Bienville, who began his language tuition in 1699, by 1700 was able, according to Iberville, "to make himself understood in Bayogoula, Ouma, Chicacha, Colapissa, and in [the languages] of the three nations up the branch of the river, which are just the same language, with little difference."[32] This was not some miraculous feat of linguistic virtuosity, since all of these languages, plus Choctaw and Alabama, were very similar to one another and so mutually comprehensible that strong arguments have been made for one of the dialects—Mobilian—being a koiné or trade language at that period.[33]

It is hard to judge how methodically mature learners like Bienville proceeded in their learning; we know that he jotted down new words as he heard them,[34] and the missionary priest Father Du Ru may have pursued the same method in learning from his aged Bayougoula tutor.[35] This was doubtless not a perfect procedure, and so laborious for serious purposes that in the later years of the colony, missionaries who needed to make use of Indian languages in complex and subtle ways were sometimes advised to use interpreters and sometimes did,[36] but it could give a rough and ready grasp of the main topics of conversation fairly quickly. The ship's carpenter and diarist Pénicaut claimed to have learned the Indian languages of the lower Mississippi and Gulf Coast regions "tolerably well" in five years; though he admitted that Mobilian alone went a long way, he also claimed to have learned Natchez, a distantly related but not mutually intelligible language.[37] Doubtless many of the other young men sent to live among the Indians during those years[38] took the opportunity to learn something, since the earliest properly-employed interpreters who appear on the census lists are neither officers nor particularly young. Occasionally, especially at the more distant posts, soldiers or traders would be encouraged to prepare as interpreters.[39]

The way the interpreter institution worked can best be demonstrated by the presentation of several representative examples for each of the major roles the interpreters filled. Its primary importance was for Indian diplomacy, and this was where the interpreter earned his subvention and his title of "Interpreter for the King." Interpreters played their most ceremonial role at the annual present-giving ceremony held by the French in Mobile. The custom of exchanging presents to cement trading and alliance relationships was an Indian one, learned by the French in Canada and adopted from the beginning in Louisiana, gaining a particular importance since it countered the English traders from the southern colonies, who gave no presents.[40] Another aspect of the presents was that the French hoped to use them to manipulate tribal power structures to assure Indian alliances.[41] This was a mutual present-giving between French and Indian; although peculating officials seldom mention the presents they received on these occasions from the Indians, presents were truly exchanged, although the King paid for the Indian presents and the officials kept those they received.[42]

Throughout the history of the presents they were nearly always presented at Mobile. The Louisiana governor would come from New Orleans with his entourage, and the Choctaw, Alabama, and sometimes other chiefs would come from their villages with their entourages. The Indians would camp outside of Mobile and the business of the presents would be held in a special barrack-like building built for that purpose. For the presents were not simply handed over; there was much ceremony—sometimes weeks of it—to be got through, and it was here that the interpreters came into their own.

Speechmaking was an important component of diplomacy from the Indian point of view, the more so as their view of negotiations was a consensual one that granted everyone the right to be heard so that leaders could detect the sense of the meeting. This is why the occasion of the presents became so dreaded by the French officials for the length and repetitiveness of the "Indian harangues," as they called these speeches. A primary duty of the interpreters, of course, was to translate these speeches in their entirety. Not so widely recognized is the fact that a scrivener was at hand to copy down what the interpreter said, and the interpreter later had to review, verify, and sign this document.

Few such actual documents with specific interpreter attributions survive from the colonly's early period, but two examples toward the end of its history and under other circumstances certainly reflect usual practice: the Flemish merchant Grevemberg's 1756 translation of the "harangues" of Quapaw chiefs demanding clemency for French deserters[43] and the signature of the King's interpreter Favré on the French text of the joint speech of d'Abbadie and Farmar in 1763 explaining the cession of eastern Louisiana to England.[44] In the former case, the document represents what the Indians said and the interpreter swears to its authenticity; in the latter, the document is the text from which he interpreted and he swears to having done so correctly.

French officials were quite aware of the fact that they were expected to respond to the "harangues," and at length. The Indians did not find it strange for the interpreter to speak for the French governor or other official, since chiefs commonly appointed skilled speakers to present their views for them. More of these governors' speeches come down to us than do those of the

Indians. A rare collection of these, copies of speeches sent to the posts by Vaudreuil for delivery by interpreters, survives in Vaudreuil's Mobile District letterbook for 1743–47.[45] They reveal a more indirect but quite indelible indication of the importance of interpreters. The self-conscious effort by Vaudreuil to cast these speeches in the Indian idiom which characterizes these texts was not peculiar to him. Speeches of the other governors are harder to find, but all reflect this artificial "Indian speech idiom." A written Bienville speech that was to be interpreted to the Natchez (whose language he did *not* speak)[46], is also cast in "Indian speech" phraseology. A speech sent by governor Périer to the Choctaw and delivered by Périer's interpreter Domingue uses it also,[47] though Périer spoke no Indian language. Thus it seems that the speech writers, and not the interpreters, were immediately responsible for the tone and idiom of the speeches by Frenchmen to Indians as preserved in the documents. It should be remembered, however, that by the time Louisiana was settled, "Indian speech idiom" was already a stylistic device, and that it ultimately derived from Canadian interpreters' word-for-word translations.

More important for the long-term effectiveness of French Indian policy was the less formal everyday role played by interpreters who were part of the garrisons of Louisiana posts. Less attention has been paid to life at the posts than is warranted, since the posts of Louisiana were the front line of Indian contacts. Most important east of the Mississippi were the Toulouse and Tombecbé forts, located at the present locations of Montgomery and Epes, Alabama, respectively. Daily contact with the Indians mostly meant trade. The posts were constantly in want of food, so they traded with the Indians for corn and meat, sometimes using trade goods officially conveyed to the posts for that purpose, sometimes using trade goods brought privately by a soldier or officer. Indians were hired explicitly to hunt for the posts, and paid in merchandise; occasionally trade was for more surprising items, like Indian pottery vessels. And after the retrocession of

Louisiana to the crown in 1732, the posts were made the official depots of deerskins for the trade, and contained warehouses to hold the deerskins and the trade goods.[48] In this environment the interpreter was in demand to assist with these exchanges.[49] Often the interpreter at a post was also a soldier, warehouse-keeper, or trader.[50]

The "indispensability" of post interpreters can also be explained by the work that had to be done to facilitate military preparations made at the posts, which invariably involved the support of Indian allies in client warfare activities against Indians allied with the English. Whenever a detachment was to be sent out in support of Indian warriors, the interpreter was first used to notify the Indians of the appointed rendezvous and to convey to the post commander the needs of the Indians in the way of ammunition for the mission. It is difficult, however, to determine where the interpreters originate in such cases. Although it is certain that an interpreter resided in Mobile and that there was one most of the time at Tombecbé fort on the Tombigbee, there are too many references to interpreters actually residing among the Choctaw to ignore. Thus when, for example, the young officer Deléry was sent to carry Bienville's "word" for the Choctaw to attack the Chickasaw in 1737, Bienville noted that although Deléry knew Choctaw,[51] he would be assisted by "the two interpreters of the nation," who "have grown up with the Indians."[52] And there are two references to the existence of Choctaw interpreters in the nation on a long-term basis: a memoir of 1726 stated that there had been an interpreter there "for twenty years,"[53] while in 1732 Father Baudouin, a capable Choctaw speaker himself, mentioned an interpreter who had spent "twenty-five or thirty years" among the Choctaw.[54] Such a continuing presence would provide substantial reinforcement to the influence of the missionary, who at that date had only been established for four years.

Interpreters who were part of a military garrison could also be sent on detachment to accompany officers and men undertaking

military or non-military tasks that involved Indian allies. Military
tasks were usually the accompanying of a small detachment of
Frenchmen who had been requested by the Indians to lead them
as they undertook client warfare against mutual enemies, but
they could be on a larger scale too, as Bienville's two Chickasaw
wars in 1736 and 1740.[55] The Choctaws were always reluctant to
undertake pure client warfare, and either insisted upon being
accompanied by Frenchmen or failed to fulfill French intentions
when they lacked such accompaniment. Accordingly, the French
usually sent eager young subalterns to join Choctaw raiding
parties when they felt that something crucial was at stake. Some
of these young men could speak the Indian language themselves:
Deléry, active during and after the 1736 Chickasaw war;[56] Le
Sueur, who led Choctaw allies against the Natchez after the 1729
revolt and later commanded Tombecbé fort;[57] Canelle, Verbois,
and Chambly, who were active in leading raids on the Chickasaws
during the early 1740s.[58] But interpreters were also used in such
forays, sometimes at risk of their lives, as when the Natchez
language interpreter, sent before the Natchez fort under a flag of
truce to summon the rebels to surrender in 1730, "was driven
back by heavy firing which made him abandon the flag."[59]

Non-military tasks for interpreters could include, for example,
escorting a party making explorations or setting up a trade house.
Knowledge of the interior grew over the century because ex-
plorers, generally engineer/surveyors, crossed and recrossed it
improving French knowledge of the location of rivers and other
important natural features as well as the location of Indian villages. The ire of the Mobile post commander, Diron d'Artaguette, was raised in 1729–1732 by the activities of Régis du
Roullet on behalf of the governor, Périer. In 1729 Régis was sent
out with one Domingue, Périer's personal interpreter, to investigate complaints of traders among the Choctaw and, in spite of
Diron's holding a grant of the Choctaw trade monopoly, to map
the major rivers of the Choctaw homeland and to investigate
possible locations for placement of a trading post within the

Choctaw nation.[60] Interestingly, Périer's interpreter brought from New Orleans was found to be competent only in the Six-towns dialect,[61] that of the southernmost division of the nation, and Régis eventually had to obtain help from Huché and Allain, the two Choctaw interpreters based at Mobile, in his foundation of a trade house and his exploration of the Pearl River.[62] Eventually he was given an interpreter of his own at the Yowani post he founded, a young drummer boy who had doubtless been fostered among the Indians in the usual way.[63]

Less visible but far more important was the aid that interpreters gave to important officers sent among the Indians to conduct diplomacy. Two examples from crises in the colony's Indian relations demonstrate this clearly. After the disastrous Natchez revolt in 1729, having failed to hear from his commercial emmissary Régis du Roullet, Périer sent the Swiss officer Jean Christophe de Lusser into the Choctaw nation to weigh their attitude and find out which side they would support. Lusser went to meet Marc Antoine Huché of Mobile, the most experienced interpreter, at the village of Chickasawhay,[64] and the two proceeded to carry out this mission. Then in 1746, the second most serious Indian crisis for Louisiana came with the murder of three Frenchmen by pro-English Choctaws during King George's War. Vaudreuil sent the major of Mobile, Jadart de Beauchamp, in a daring move to demand the heads of the murderers, and Beauchamp was accompanied by Huché's successor in the chief interpreter post, Jean Baptiste Allain *dit* Roussève.[65] Both Lusser and Beauchamp spoke some Choctaw, and in neither case does the interpreter figure prominently in their reports; nevertheless in both cases only the best interpreter would do. It should be pointed out, too, that in both cases the officers took advantage of the presence and aid of Father Baudouin, the missionary to the Choctaw who was so well-versed in their language and culture.[66]

Sometimes, too, interpreters would be specifically sent on their own to carry out diplomatic missions. Usually this would entail the presentation of a speech to an Indian gathering on behalf of some French official; such was the way Vaudreuil's collection of speeches mentioned above was delivered, and quite often he specifies that a speech is to be delivered by an interpreter.[67] These speeches were not, however, merely delivered. As Vaudreuil specifies at one point, the interpreter was to modify the speech in accordance with local conditions and the Indian responses to the speeches were to be written down article by article on the margin of the speech.[68] That this was a usual practice is demonstrated by the existence of a set of instructions given by Périer in 1729 with responses written down by Huché as he dealt with the Choctaw according to those instructions.[69]

At other times interpreters could be sent more privately to attempt to influence some important chief or faction leader. Sometimes there was active incitement to violence, as when the Choctaw interpreter induced a loyal chief to kill an English trader in 1726.[70] More often the interpreter served as a French presence and simply backed the views of the pro-French faction in council deliberations.[71]

Such activities come very close to falling into the category of spying or intelligence-gathering, which was one of the interpreter's most important roles. As intelligence gatherers, interpreters were uniquely suited to disentangle the maze of Indian names, the complex relationships among Indian villages, and the subtleties of Indian internal politics. It was not unusual for the interpreters to use their knowledge of Indian language and culture to go "undercover" to gather intelligence. Thus Huché was sent to socialize with some Chickasaw guests in the Choctaw village of Scanapa to discover their intentions in 1730;[72] thus the interpreter at Fort Toulouse eavesdropped on discussions between local Alabamas and visiting Choctaws.[73] A talent for *bonhomie* was apparently helpful. Vaudreuil praised a certain Gaspard, probably a trader/interpreter, for his ability to gather information from inebriated Indians.[74] Finally, there were out-and-out spy missions. In 1736, preparing to attack a Chakchiuma village with Tunica allies, Petit de Livilliers sent in his interpreter to size up the situation. "This Frenchman was received as a trader who wished to buy grain. He visited all the cabins, counted all the warriors, and when the night was well advanced he slipped out of the village. . ."[75]

Cursed with a population that was always smaller than was healthy, the French were very concerned to be kept up to date about the facts of Indian demographics, particularly how many warriors a given village or tribe could field. On the commercial side, it was also valuable to know about population distributions in order to anticipate and even court markets. The evidence suggests that interpreters made periodic journeys through all the villages of a tribe with the gathering of just such information in mind. The same kind of tour of an Indian nation could also provide an assessment of its mood, and the interpreters were frequently called upon to gather this kind of information too. This would be done through a series of more or less casual visits to friendly chiefs and a few native spies. Both purposes would be served by a written report to post commander or governor. Such assessments were vital to the French desire to predict what the Indians would do in a given situation, although only rarely are they preserved.[76] Two of the most well-known of such reports were prepared by Régis du Roullet and Jean Christophe de Lusser in 1729 and 1730,[77] and though these men were officers and not interpreters, their work depended crucially on the four interpreters who worked with them: Huché and Allain from Mobile and Domingue and the drummer boy from New Orleans. Huché is specifically credited with having sent back written reports to Régis, who incorporated them in his own work.[78] That interpreters did provide written reports of their intelligence-gathering among the Indians is indicated by the mention of a copy of a journal kept by Allain in 1745.[79]

This discussion of roles and the personnel who were sent to fill them provides apparent formulae that traduce the individualism that resulted from the "formation" of an interpreter by the French method. The resulting product pursued a relatively unusual lifestyle, yet made himself an integral part of native and colonial society alike. The lessons of Canada had shown not only that the interpreters were likely to go native, but that much was a desirable outcome from the point of view of French success in Indian diplomacy. Thus although there was not overt encouragement of an adoption of Indian lifestyle, neither was such a choice penalized, by government or church.

One key element in the native acculturation of interpreter candidates was their fictive adoption by Indian sponsors, usually chiefs of some standing. Such adoption is suggested by the early request by the Indians for young boys to learn their languages, and we know in several cases that it certainly happened. In one instance, indeed, that of a boy orphaned in the Natchez uprising of 1729, the Indian who had ransomed him from his Natchez captors, being offered only a single blanket as a reward for his return, "had preferred to bring him back rather than surrender him for so little, saying that he would adopt him as his nephew."[80] It seems likely that the chiefs who asked for French boys intended a similar adoption since there were aboriginal precedents for the advantages to be gained by such an action.

The meaning of this fictive adoption was not only that the boy would enjoy the role, perquisites, and duties of whatever position in the kinship network he had been adopted into, but more importantly, it may have been a formal part of the Indian notion of intergroup diplomacy. The institution of the *fanimingo* among the Chickasaw and Choctaw is relevant here: members of a foreign tribe or kinship group would adopt a member of another, providing him with hospitality and presents and giving him a significant kinship role. In return, he was to represent them in the councils of his own people, to argue their concerns and make their worthiness known. I have shown elsewhere[81] that French officialdom did not understand or make use of this institution, but it may be that in adopting as their *fanimingo* a young man who was preparing to be what Indians viewed as the chief's speaker, the Indians thought they were applying this institution cross-culturally.

It was not unlikely that French boys reaching puberty while living among Indian tribes and sharing their values would seek sexual relationships with Indian women. Certainly the Canadians who were bivouacked among the Indians in the early days of the colony did so, and some of these latter relationships became permanent marriages sanctioned by the church.[82] The significance of such marriages was great and positive for French diplomacy, since any offspring, in the matrilineal societies of the southeast, were considered fully Indian and of the tribe of the mother, while their affectionate and nonauthoritarian relationship with their French father would further encourage the friendly relationship. It is not clear whether any of the official interpreters of the colony married into native groups, but it is certain that their friends did—notably the settler Baudrau *dit* Graveline and the officer Juzan.[83] There is strong cause for presumption that the interpreter Simon Favré, so influential in the latter years of the colony,[84] may have had a second family that founded the large and influential Mississippi Choctaw Farve line.

Many if not most of the interpreters carried on a private Indian trade on their own account, on much the same footing as the civilian Indian traders. They had good reason to do so. The pay of interpreters was not high: it ranged from 300 to 600 livres/year, apparently at random, which was a fraction of what officers received (see Table 1). Since most of the interpreters had families, some of them large, they were expected to do some trading on their own account.[85] During the 1730s Huché, previously Diron d'Artaguette's interpreter/trader among the Choctaw, was put in charge of the Choctaw trade warehouses within the nation,[86] and after 1745 Allain *dit* Rousséve was granted a monopoly of the skin trade at Mobile.[87] Intertribal trading relationships in the whole of aboriginal America were commonly cemented by fictive adoptions, so the carrying on of trade by an interpreter who was adopted and/or married into a tribe was very much in tune with Indian tradition. He would not have to worry about the vicissitudes of European competition for Indian favor, since he

TABLE 1   Louisiana Interpreter Salaries

Year	Salary	Remarks	Source
1713	360 livres/yr.	Old Mobile	C13A, 3:288
1716	360 livres/yr.	Old Mobile	C13A, 4:766v–767
1721	500 livres/yr.	Mobile; + 2 rations	C13A, 6:147
1723	300 livres/yr.	Toulouse; in merchandise	C13A, 7:119
1723	200 livres/yr.	Natchez; in merchandise	C13A, 7:124
1725	600 livres/yr.	Illinois	C13A, 9:84v
1725	300 livres/yr.	New Orleans; + rations	C13A, 9:145v
1734	600 livres/yr.	Natchez	C13A, 18:33–33bis
1734	400 livres/yr.	Illinois	C13A, 18:34v

had in effect become an Indian himself; nor did he have to worry about the safety of his trade goods within his adopted village in his absence. With such advantages it is not surprising that several of the interpreters managed eventually to become very prosperous.

Thus the acculturated interpreter, in his role of proxy diplomatist and trader, was in an ideal position to act as a cultural broker between Indian and European: he understood both the material aspects of the two cultures and the attitudes that articulated them. Perhaps he could even see and suggest solutions to the problems of contact that would not even occur to one who did not see both sides. What happened to the interpreter himself in this process was that he had to stand between the two cultures for the rest of his life.

The relationship of the interpreters and their families to the French community was therefore somewhat anomalous. In their work they dealt most directly with officers and high-ranking officials of the colony, yet a good portion of the rest of their time was spent in the Indian villages, and that side of their lives apparently precluded them from participation in the finer circles of Louisiana society. For most this was probably not a hardship. The pathetic social posturings of backwoods officials aping the class prejudices of France must have seemed as hollow as they actually were when compared with the relatively classless merit-based Indian ranking system. The contrast could often lead to repugnance for the French system, as was clearly the case with the interpreter Huché when he told Régis du Roullet that he did not wish to set up his household in the French compound Régis was building in the Yowani village, but preferred to take a cabin within the Indian village to house the family he had brought with him from Mobile. "This life," Régis reported disgustedly, "pleases him and he would not give it up for a great deal. . ."[88]

Yet standing of the Indian interpreters in the French communities that were at least their part-time bases was reasonably good. An examination of the marriage records of Mobile, where the chief Choctaw interpreters were based, shows that they found friends and acquaintances among the families of small merchants and plantation owners; they did not participate in the high society of high-ranking officers and civil officials, but neither were their friends the soldiers and workmen of the colony. The best description of their milieu was that of settlers, *habitants:* people who were casting their lot seriously with the colony, who married fellow creoles in the second generation instead of sending for wives from France and who all had country plantations. But perhaps understandably, their closest relations within the French community were with each other—they married sisters and cousins, their children married each other.[89] Thus Marc Antoine Huché, the first full-time interpreter to appear in the colony's records by name,[90] was apparently a friend of Pierre Allain *dit* Rousséve, a blacksmith.[91] Pierre's son, Jean-Baptiste Allain *dit* Rousséve, became a protégé of Huché, married a girl who may have been his stepdaughter, and succeeded him as chief Choctaw interpreter around 1730–1732.[92] By the 1740s, Jean-Baptiste's son, Jean-Baptiste Rousséve *dit* Allain, was active as an interpreter.[93] The Favré family begins to show up in the records in the

1740s also, and they are friendly with the Juzans, already a mixed-blood family, who are in turn friendly with the Roussèves. A Favré son marries yet another of the ubiquitous Colon girls in 1759, witnessed by Pierre Juzan and Jean-Baptiste Roussève.

At this distance in time it is hard to judge the extent to which this small circle of interpreter families was turned in upon itself by external pressure. Saving the posturings of Louisiana society's leading lights, the new colony's social habits seem to have been fairly relaxed and its restraints few. If the interpreters kept to themselves, perhaps it was that they chose to do so, a cultural *métis* between two worlds but belonging to neither.

The Southern Colonies: A General Perspective

ROBERT MIDDLEKAUFF

My assignment is to assess the papers we have heard, and to offer suggestions about them and the possibilities of future research. I do so with considerable hesitation—even reluctance—because I am not an historian of the southern colonies. Professor Jordan reassured me some time ago, by saying that a fresh perspective is needed and at times, at least, an outsider (a non-specialist) has such a perspective. I fear that freshness born of ignorance has its limitations, but I offer these comments nonetheless.

Galloway

Dr. Galloway's paper explores a fresh line of study of Indian-white relations. Because it deals with French Louisiana, it at first may not seem to have importance for the English colonies. Dr. Galloway presents in clear focus a pattern of relationships important for diplomacy and the social circumstances of a group that did not exist in the English colonies. What happened in the English colonies was different, and we can understand it better as a result of learning about French Louisiana. This judgment is from a provincial perspective of course—what happened in a French colony has importance for itself—and not just for what it sets in relief in the English colonies.

There were mixed bloods along the frontier of the British southern colonies. My impression is that their accommodation with prevailing society to the east was not easily accomplished or ever complete. In French Louisiana, Dr. Galloway suggests, the second generation of interpreter families stayed within themselves. They were caught, she says, between two worlds: that of established French Louisiana society and that of the Indians.

131

They apparently stayed pretty much to themselves, perhaps by choice. Yet they and their fathers performed a useful function and were recognized by both white and red men for their utility.

Early in her paper Dr. Galloway refers to the question of general French attitudes toward the Indian. There is a body of scholarship on this matter (some is cited in Dr. Galloway's notes). One would like to know what in this scholarship seems valuable to Dr. Galloway, and what questions she believes ought to be pursued. She suggests that "it can be fairly argued" that French attitudes "were noticeably less racist." Her paper and the evidence she provides surely substantiate that judgment. What accounts for the French attitude is a worthy question, especially since the French, as Dr. Galloway shows, were certainly as "exploitative" as other Europeans.

Dr. Galloway's paper is intriguing and lucid in every respect. It almost demands that another step of analysis be taken: comparison with English and Spanish experience. It is worth noting here that Professor Menard's paper contains data on the difficulty of enslaving Indians in the Carolina Lowcountry.

Menard

Mr. Menard's paper—"The Rise of Plantation Society in the Carolina Lowcountry"—is simply superb. It is not about plantation society in the broad sense, but about the development of the labor force in the Lowcountry. The history of this development is skillfully reconstructed. The Gemery-Hogendorn model, which Menard carefully cites, has not been one of the staples of historical discourse, though it may become one. In the book, *The Economy of British America, 1607–1789*, McCusker and Menard explain further the strengths and weaknesses of Gemery-Hogendorn.[1] Evaluating Professor Menard's manipulation of the model in the technical sense is beyond my powers of analysis. But still I find his use of the model helpful and convincing. The most reassuring feature of Professor Menard's application of Gemery-Hogendorn is his insistence that something beyond "flow" and the elasticities of supply be considered. He introduces circumstances we might call "cultural"—for example the Lowcountry planters' attitudes towards women, attitudes that made them reluctant to employ white women in the fields. And—one more example—"In the eighteenth century, as racial attitudes hardened, one also encounters sentiments expressing a reluctance to employ whites in tasks identified with blacks."

The center of Professor Menard's paper is the history of the Carolina labor force—and two processes: 1) from white servants to slaves; and 2) from Indian slaves and blacks from the West Indies to African slaves (or African sources). His account of both processes is well-told. The explanation he offers of the two transitions—from servants to slaves and from West Indian slaves to African slaves—is convincing and enlightening, and I admire his insightful comments on enslaved Indians and his weaving together of the data of trade, population, and market demand.

Perhaps there is one missing element—one piece of data. Perhaps, Professor Menard simply assumes it as a given. I refer to white attitudes towards blacks, to racism in other words. The first transition he describes—from servitude to slavery is only fully comprehensible if one assumes the existence of racism. Professor Menard ties together many aspects of the history of the Carolina Lowcountry. He refers to planter preferences at several points. Those preferences were in part shaped by demographic and economic circumstances. In part they were cultural. That fact, I believe, needs some explicit recognition.

Smith

The papers of Professors Smith and Morgan are related in theme and interest. Both are concerned with "patriarchialism" and families. Professor Smith wishes to locate the southern colonial family in a broad way within the broader social order, to see it in relationship to a gradually emerging society that took on some stability. For the seventeenth century he emphasizes the disorderly and disordered character of southern social life—with sex ratios unbalanced, mortality rates high, with many new migrants living alone rather than in families. He notes the prevalence of widows and orphans everywhere. By the early eighteenth century, something approaching a stable, patriarchal family system was emerging. This system "derived from" increased life expectancy, the development of a native-born society, and the large-scale introduction of slave labor.

On the inner life of families, as he says, not much is known. He has suggestive points to make about William Byrd of Westover, in particular Byrd's conduct midst the varieties of his dependents which indicates that Byrd saw family life as a public phenomenon, marked by a constant sociability and companionship. Byrd's round of activities stood in clear contrast to the realities of his own family life which was filled with quarrels, whippings of slaves, and an indiscriminate aggressiveness.

There are dangers in discussing "the colonial family in the southern colonies" without taking great care in establishing the social contest. Although I know that Professor Smith recognized the danger, he does not altogether escape it. His distinction between the families of the gentry and others is very broad. It may be that regional variations should be noted: the conventional categories of southern colonial life—Tidewater and backcountry, Chesapeake and Carolinas, and so on may be helpful. Or may not. The attention Professor Smith pays to patriarchy and paternalism suggests that social class ought to be given more consideration, if Gene Genovese (who uses paternalism in a different sense) is correct.

But all of these are very large categories, and it is unfair to ask Mr. Smith to write a paper as if it were a book. What he has done is admirable. He has taken a large subject, and he has had the daring to paint his historical picture with very broad strokes.

There is a poignancy in his conclusions about the importance of recapturing something of inner experience, the experience of the individual in the family. I will leave his paper with several questions; in a sense all that I am going to ask him is to explain further.

What does he want to know about individual experience in the family? Is there some common thread of the experience of children and parents? Why is such knowledge important? And in what sense? Is there any way to relate this experience to the role of the family in the social order?

Morgan

Professor Morgan wishes to establish something about the nature of the transitions from patriarchalism to paternalism. I am not altogether clear what he means by either of these terms. But I believe he means to describe rather formal, even inflexible social relations by the first term (patriarchalism), and something looser, perhaps more personal by the term paternalism. The cases of master-slave relationships he describes—Carter, Laurens, Thistlewood—all lend themselves to this interpretation.

The differences in Morgan's three cases are great, but the essential similarities are clear and surely important for an understanding of the nature of slavery. It is proper to be concerned with differences in patterns of slavery—after all it was not a static institution. Perhaps a non-specialist's perspective might be helpful in understanding slavery in its deepest character. Slavery involved the ownership of one human being by another, and wherever it existed, force and the power to take life lay at its roots. This power may not have been expressed often, but it was there. In the usual round of existence, in normal circumstances in each of these societies the exercise of power was curtailed, or restricted (broadly speaking) by culture. In particular—and most commonly—that part of culture defined by the economic interests of the planter. Whatever else it was, slavery was a method of organizing and using a labor force. And that labor had a common value. It was not ordinarily in the interest of any of these three— Carter, Laurens, Thistlewood—to destroy their slaves.

The other aspects of culture—the culture of the slave as well as the master—are alluded to, or hinted at, by Dr. Morgan. What transpired in the relations of these masters and their slaves was conditioned by their cultures.

Let me say just a few words about that—to give some concreteness to these general propositions. Consider Carter: we know from his diary that he lived by an ethic that began with the assumption that man was imperfect, but that he could be improved. Carter really did not feel warmly disposed towards human kind in the abstract—or in the flesh. He really did not think too much of himself. But he was relentless in his desire for improvement—especially in others. He may not have accorded slaves a full place among the human species, but he certainly expected them to conduct themselves according to certain standards. Dr. Morgan tells us of Carter's disappointment in Nassau, who drank to excess. Carter once went so far as to confess his disappointment about Nassau in the *Virginia Gazette*. Yet, he kept him though he often resolved to sell him.

Carter always felt some ambivalence towards his slaves, as Dr. Morgan says in recounting Carter's experience with skilled slaves, elderly slaves, his dramatic concern for their health, his recognition of their need for families. All this sets Carter slightly apart from "the traditional patriarchal mode of domination," Dr. Morgan says.

Dr. Morgan means to expose more of the traditional mode of domination in discussing Laurens and Thistlewood. Certainly the examples of slave life he gives in South Carolina and Jamaica are harsh—the domination is severe, even barbarous in Thistlewood's Jamaica.

In thinking about these three cases, I am impressed by the varieties of behavior of both masters and slaves, and of the varieties of social circumstances of each. Carter is a planter on the scene; Laurens, a merchant-planter usually at some distance from most of his slaves; and Thistlewood, first an estate manager and then finally a provisioning planter but not a sugar magnate. Dr. Morgan points out all this with thoroughness and care. Yet he also seems to find value in thinking of these men, as evidently they thought of themselves, in terms of patriarchalism. It is certainly an elastic term, especially when one considers the varieties of discipline used by these three.

Carter was most like a patriarch within his immediate family, especially in his relations with his sons, Ralph Wormeley and John. In dealing with these two, Carter's religious faith was much in evidence. Ralph Wormeley aroused his fears for his salvation by leading what appeared clearly to his father a dissolute life, complete with an addiction to cards, an aversion to work, and a fondness for strong drink. The father tried everything to bring the son under control—he threatened him, advised him, reasoned with him, and almost bribed him. Carter wanted to save his son's soul he tells his diary in December 1774, but he failed.[2]

Even by the standards of eighteenth-century patriarchalism, Carter was an oppressive father. To assess Carter's experience with his slaves, one might find additional evidence in his tortured relations with his sons. Certainly these relations give perspectives on Carter and his chattels.

One may doubt, or at least question, the value of patriarchalism as an interpretative device. These planters studied by Dr. Morgan used another language as well as the one drawn from patriarchal conceptions. This second language was the language of commerce. There is much in the sources about bargains, negotiations, and contracts. Masters negotiated with slaves, and they fashioned contracts to define their relations. Such words, and the conceptions that underlay them, came naturally to the tongues of planters. They were businessmen as well as patriarchs. The way they expressed themselves suggests that they thought of themselves in several ways, suggests indeed that their behavior and their conceptions of themselves may at times have been at odds.

Tate

Dr. Tate's general survey is enlightening, and one can only admire his command of the literature of the field. His point about southern regionalism is valuable as are his detailed comments on changes in historiography. Tate's generous view of his subject—his catholicity of mind—is unusual in these days of specialization. One hopes that others will follow his example.

The Need for a Comparative Perspective

All of these essays are suggestive. Considered together they lead one to think more generally about the southern colonies and to offer several larger propositions about their study.

Focusing on the southern colonies is useful and fruitful of knowledge. But in studying the particular, or the part of a whole, the context of study is a powerful condition in forming historical understanding. At times the context becomes clearer when comparisons are made. Every event, of course, has its own context, and to some extent most written history is comparative. Understandably the comparisons made in these essays have not been broad, and they have not carried the discussion much beyond the American mainland.

The southern colonies as Thad Tate has argued, were a part of the British Empire. But he seems to believe that there is limited value in seeing these colonies in an imperial context. The limitations of the imperial context are real, but the southern colonies were an extension of Europe and Africa, and the political center of their universe before the eighteenth century was England as much as it was America. By implication at least, Tate's essay and the others concentrate on what set the colonies apart from the Empire.

The essays do not recognize that the southern colonies, for all their difference from the colonies to the north, also shared much with them. There are analogies or echoes to the north, for example, of the disorder and disruption of seventeenth-century southern colonial families. The strife and upheaval were clearest in the social and religious experience of New England. Thanks to the researches of David Lovejoy, Philip Gura and others, we know much about the enthusiasm that frequently shattered the standing order of Massachusetts Bay, Connecticut, and Rhode Island.[3] "The World Turned Upside Down," Christopher Hill's phrase, describes phenomena not only of Civil War England, but also of a variety of American colonies in the seventeenth and eighteenth centuries, including surely the backcountry of the southern colonies, the old New England colonies, and at times Pennsylvania and New Jersey.

To extend this comparison into politics and governance is not difficult. Problems of governance plagued virtually all of the American mainland colonies in the seventeenth century. The Dominion of New England, and the revolution that destroyed it is only one example. At almost the same time, Leisler's Rebellion shook New York. I do not mean to suggest that there was a perfect parallel in the political experience of northern and southern colonies, but the upheaval that cursed life in the southern colonies had its shadow in those to the north. (One of the things that set New England apart, of course, was a greater stability in the family, and I do not wish to press comparisons too far.)

As a further point of comparison, it is worth remarking on the existence of representative forms of government in all of the colonies—north and south. This comparison is obvious and extremely important for the understanding of the American Revolution. There were differences in institutions from colony to colony; yet while legislatures followed various lines of development, the similarities cut deeper.

To some extent familial politics was found in almost all the mainland colonies. Dr. Smith properly emphasizes the growth of family dynasties in southern colonial political life. We should not overlook similar cases to the north—the Delanceys, Livingstons, Schuylers in New York, for example, and the Winthrops in Massachusetts.

What of education and, in particular, female education? The eighteenth-century ideal in Virginia was the genteel lady, according to Smith. He tells us that this was the society that launched sons and polished daughters. The sons of the gentry read the classics. So also did the sons of a similar group in the colonies to the north.

As for the daughters of the gentry: Mary Ambler's attitudes, as cited by Smith, seem similar to many held farther to the north. Mary Ambler urged her daughter to heed a sermon which recommended the joining of the "natural softness" of the young lady to "christian meekness." The sermon was indistinguishable from others preached to the daughters of mainland gentry in the eighteenth century. And the recommended course of study—dancing, drawing, and the other gentle arts, and solid christian teaching—was the stuff of ordinary practice. The ideal was to polish the surface of a sanctified substance.

Few, if any, in the colonies made a claim for the equality of women. The genteel ideal prescribed a regime in which a young woman would cultivate certain of the arts with the intention of developing her finer side. History, biography, and memoirs were often recommended in order to provide a girl with models of virtue which she could emulate and vices she could shun. She might read travel accounts to improve her mind. With a knowledge of the arts and of virtue, she might serve not merely as a household drudge or as a purveyor of traditional morality, but also as a companion to her husband, lighting his life with charm and sensibility. Thus the theory ennobled women while reaffirming her inferiority. The purpose of her education remained what it had always been: to help her serve in a world made for men.

Not only in education, but in much else, genteel culture everywhere in the colonies shared common values. The differences between Chesapeake planters and New England merchant-landowners was great of course. But there was in common a confidence in the rightness of their leadership and a sense that they had a responsible role to play in public life. By the time of the Revolution, "virtue" meant the same thing to gentry everywhere in America; and so did "corruption," "power," and "liberty." We need studies of the gentry in all of the colonies—local, regional studies, and more to the point of what I am saying, comparative studies.

The religion of the southern colonies has received much study, especially the church. Yet much more needs to be learned. Rhys Isaac has recently described evangelical culture in Virginia.[4] Surely a broader focus is needed. My intention here is to suggest that the commonalities of evangelical culture in the mainland colonies—north and south—require assessment. To be sure there were interesting, perhaps fundamental differences between the practice of religion in the northern and southern colonies. A congregational democracy flourished in the middle and New England colonies in the eighteenth century; it made little headway in the established church in Virginia. Yet the evangelists were in many respects practicing democrats.

To explore these interesting matters, a broad comparative perspective is needed. Local and regional studies promise much—and deliver much—as Thad Tate has shown. Tate finds value in much recent study which, he argues, compels us to look forward rather than backward. He points to the linkages that run from the southern colonies to the later South. He is right about this tendency.

Yet, while historians look at the southern colonies, they might profitably look elsewhere in the colonial world. Winthrop Jordan's magnificent book, *White Over Black,* ought to be a model. And, of course, there are others which treat slavery in an even broader perspective.[5]

There are dangers in looking into the nineteenth century when one's purpose is to reconstruct the culture of the seventeenth and eighteenth centuries. In recent years the danger had been especially clear in scholarly study of New England towns. Kenneth Lockridge's study of Dedham looks to explain the passage of a town from a closed corporate community to democracy and individualism. This theme, interesting as it is, may obscure or skew perceptions of local realities.

So there is a danger. A book that transcends it is Edmund S. Morgan's *American Slavery, American Freedom: The Ordeal of Colonial Virginia.*[6] Morgan provides a powerful social history of seventeenth-century Virginia, explains the affinities linking slavery and freedom, and thereby suggests something of the historical origins of American democracy. Models are useful; and they are stimulating. But there is no substitute for imagination. The symposium that produced these essays offers a reassuring example of imaginations at work. The essays give promise that much more will be accomplished.

Notes

Notes to INTRODUCTION

1. John Richard Alden, *The First South* (Baton Rouge, Louisiana State University Press, 1961).
2. Max Farrand, ed., *The Records of the Federal Convention of 1787*, rev. ed., 4 vols. (New Haven, Yale University Press, 1937), vol. 2, pp. 9–10; also vol. 1, p. 476.
3. Winthrop D. Jordan, *White Over Black: American Attitudes Toward the Negro, 1550–1812* (Chapel Hill, University of North Carolina Press, 1968), pp. 315–316, 345.

Notes to DEFINING THE COLONIAL SOUTH
by Thad W. Tate

1. Wesley Frank Craven, *The Southern Colonies in the Seventeenth Century, 1607–1689* (Baton Rouge, Louisiana State University Press, 1949), p. xiii.
2. Thomas Jefferson Wertenbaker, *The Old South: The Founding of American Civilization* (New York, Scribner, 1942); Clarence L. Ver Steeg, *Origins of a Southern Mosaic: Studies of Early Carolina and Georgia* (Athens, University of Georgia Press, 1975); Allan Kulikoff, *Tobacco and Slaves: The Development of Southern Cultures in the Chesapeake, 1600–1800* (Chapel Hill, University of North Carolina Press, 1986), pp. 421–436.
3. "Outside the Groove of History," (unpublished paper) Southern Historical Association, 48th Annual Meeting (1982).
4. *Journal of Southern History*, 50 (February 1984): 3–14.
5. John Richard Alden, *The First South* (Baton Rouge, Louisiana State University Press, 1961).
6. Ver Steeg, *Origins of a Southern Mosaic*, p. xii.
7. Carl Bridenbaugh, *Myths & Realities; Societies of the Colonial South* (Baton Rouge, Louisiana State University Press, 1952).
8. Aubrey C. Land, "American South," *Journal of Southern History*, 50 (February 1984):14.
9. Ibid., p. 7.
10. See esp. Hugh F. Rankin, "The Colonial South," in Arthur S. Link and Rembert W. Patrick, eds., *Writing Southern History: Essays in Historiography in Honor of Fletcher M. Green* (Baton Rouge, Louisiana State University Press, 1965); Clarence L. Ver Steeg, "Historians and the Southern Colonies," in Ray Allen Billington, ed., *The Reinterpretation of Early American History: Essays in Honor of John Edwin Pomtret* (San Marino, California Huntington Library, 1966); and, most recently, George C. Rogers's essay on the pre-1800 South in John B. Boles and Evelyn Thomas Nolen, eds., *Interpreting Southern History: Historiographical Essays in Honor of Sanford W. Higginbotham* (Baton Rouge, Louisiana State University Press, 1986). Professor Rogers comments perceptively on

the problem of synthesizing the history of the early South and at the same time provides a much more complete historiographical survey than the present more exploratory essay seeks to do.

11. Charles S. Sydnor, *Gentleman Freeholders: Political Practices in Washington's Virginia* (Chapel Hill, University of North Carolina Press, 1952); Jack P. Greene, *The Quest for Power: The Lower Houses of Assembly in the Southern Royal Colonies, 1689–1776* (Chapel Hill, University of North Carolina Press, 1963); M. Eugene Sirmans, *Colonial South Carolina: A Political History, 1663–1763* (Chapel Hill, University of North Carolina Press, 1966); William W. Abbot, *The Royal Governors of Georgia, 1754–1775* (Chapel Hill, University of North Carolina Press, 1959); Wilcomb E. Washburn, *The Governor and the Rebel: A History of Bacon's Rebellion in Virginia* (Chapel Hill, University of North Carolina Press, 1957); Richard Maxwell Brown, *The South Carolina Regulators* (Cambridge, Belknap Press of Harvard University Press, 1963). Robert M. Weir's articles and essays are conveniently collected in *"The Last of American Freemen": Studies in the Political Culture of the Colonial and Revolutionary South* (Macon, Georgia, Mercer University Press, 1986).

12. "Political Development," in Jack P. Greene and J. R. Pole, eds., *Colonial British America: Essays in the New History of the Early Modern Era* (Baltimore, The Johns Hopkins University Press, 1984), pp. 435–436.

13. *White Over Black: American Attitudes Toward the Negro, 1550–1812* (Chapel Hill, University of North Carolina Press, 1968).

14. Although there is a more extensive literature, this interpretation rests particularly on Russell R. Menard, "From Servants to Slaves: The Transformation of the Chesapeake Labor System, 1680–1710," *Southern Studies*, 16 (Winter 1977):355–390.

15. The significance and character of slavery and black culture in the Chesapeake is developed most broadly in Edmund S. Morgan, *American Slavery, American Freedom: The Ordeal of Colonial Virginia* (New York, W. W. Norton, 1975); Kulikoff, *Tobacco and Slaves*, pp. 317–420; and Gerald W. [Michael] Mullin, *Flight and Rebellion: Slave Resistance in Eighteenth-Century Virginia* (New York, Oxford University Press, 1972).

16. See Peter H. Wood, *Black Majority: Negroes in Colonial South Carolina from 1670 through the Stono Rebellion* (New York, Alfred A. Knopf, 1974); Daniel C. Littlefield, *Rice and Slaves: Ethnicity and the Slave Trade in Colonial South Carolina* (Baton Rouge, Louisiana State University Press, 1981); and, pending the publication of his larger study of Afro-American culture in colonial Virginia and South Carolina, a number of significant essays by Philip D. Morgan, esp. "Work and Culture: The Task System and the World of Lowcountry Blacks, 1700–1880," *William and Mary Quarterly*, 3rd Ser., 39 (October 1982):563–599.

17. This position is effectively argued for North Carolina in the work of Michael L. M. Kay. See, e.g., "The North Carolina Regulation, 1766–1776; A Class Conflict," in Alfred F. Young, ed., *The American Revolution: Explorations in the History of American Radicalism* (Dekalb, Northern Illinois University Press, 1976), pp. 71–123. For South Carolina, see Ronald Hoffman, "The Disaffected in the Revolutionary South," in Young, ed., *American Revolution*, pp. 273–317, and Jerome J. Nadelhaft, *The Disorders of War: The Revolution in South Carolina* (Orono, University of Maine Press, 1981).

18. Brown, *South Carolina Regulators;* James P. Whittenburg, "Planters, Merchants, and Lawyers: Social Change and the Orgins of the North Carolina Regulation," *William and Mary Quarterly*, 3rd Ser., 34 (October 1977):215–238; and A.

Roger Ekrich, "The North Carolina Regulators on Liberty and Corruption, 1766–1771," *Perspectives in American History*, 11 (1977–1978):199–256.

19. Richard R. Beeman, *The Evolution of the Southern Backcountry: A Case Study of Lunenburg County, Virginia, 1746–1832* (Philadelphia, University of Pennsylvania Press, 1984); Rhys Isaac, *The Transformation of Virginia, 1740–1790* (Chapel Hill, University of North Carolina Press, 1982).

20. Rachel Klein, "Unification of a Slave State: The Rise of the Planters in the South Carolina Backcountry, 1760–1808." (unpublished manuscript). Readers will find useful her essay, "Frontier Planters and the American Revolution: The South Carolina Backcountry, 1775–1782," in Ronald Hoffman, Thad W. Tate, and Peter J. Albert, *An Uncivil War: The Southern Backcountry during the American Revolution* (Charlottesville, University Press of Virginia, 1985).

21. D. W. Meining, *The Shaping of America: A Geographical Perspective on 500 Years of History*, vol. 1, *Atlantic America, 1492–1800* (New Haven, 1986), pp. 147, 153–160, 179, 182, 225.

22. Ibid., pp. 191–254, briefly indicates some possibilities in this approach.

23. See, e.g., Allan Kulikoff, "The Colonial Chesapeake: Seedbed of Antebellum Southern Culture?," *Journal of Southern History*, 45 (November 1979):513–540.

Notes to IN SEARCH OF THE FAMILY IN THE COLONIAL SOUTH
by Daniel Blake Smith

1. See in particular, Bertram Wyatt-Brown, *Southern Honor: Ethics and Behavior in the Old South* (New York, Oxford University Press, 1982).

2. Allan Kulikoff, *Tobacco and Slaves: The Development of Southern Cultures in the Chesapeake, 1680–1800* (Chapel Hill, University of North Carolina Press, 1986), p. 35; Edmund S. Morgan, *American Slavery, American Freedom: the Ordeal of Colonial Virginia* (New York, W. W. Norton, 1975), p. 407.

3. Darrett B. and Anita H. Rutman, "'Now-Wives and Sons-in-Law': Parental Death in a Seventeenth-Century Virginia County," in Thad W. Tate and David L. Ammerman, eds., *The Chesapeake in the Seventeenth Century: Essays in Anglo-American Society* (Chapel Hill, University of North Carolina Press, 1979), pp. 153–182; Daniel Blake Smith, "Mortality and Family in the Colonial Chesapeake," *Journal of Interdisciplinary History*, 8 (Winter 1978):415.

4. Morgan, *American Slavery, American Freedom*, pp. 165–167; Kulikoff, *Tobacco and Slaves*, p. 168; Lois G. Carr and Lorena S. Walsh, "The Planter's Wife: The Experience of White Women in Seventeenth-Century Maryland," *William and Mary Quarterly*, 3rd. Ser., 34 (October 1977):542–571.

5. Lorena S. Walsh, "'Till Death Us Do Part': Marriage and Family in Seventeenth-Century Maryland," in Tate and Ammerman, eds., *The Chesapeake in the Seventeenth Century*, pp. 130–131.

6. Ibid., p. 132.

7. Darrett B. and Anita H. Rutman, *A Place in Time: Middlesex County, Virginia, 1650–1750* (New York, W. W. Norton, 1984), p. 114; Smith, "Mortality and Family," pp. 421–422.

8. The phrase "despoil the parentless" is from Rutman and Rutman, *A Place in Time*, p. 117. See also Walsh, "'Till Death Us Do Part'," pp. 135–136.

9. Gloria L. Main, *Tobacco Colony: Life in Early Maryland, 1650–1720* (Princeton, Princeton University Press, 1982), p. 265.

10. Ibid., pp. 254–258.

11. Peter Laslett, *The World We Have Lost* (New York, Scribner, 1965), pp. 98–99; Bernard Bailyn, "Politics and Social Structure in Virginia," in James Morton Smith, ed., *Seventeenth-Century America* (Chapel Hill, University of North Carolina Press, 1959), pp. 90–118; Timothy Breen, "Labor Force and Race Relations in Virginia, 1660–1710," *Journal of Social History*, 7 (Fall 1973):1–20; Edmund S. Morgan, "Slavery and Freedom: the American Paradox," *Journal of American History*, 59 (June 1972):5–30.

12. William Fitzhugh to Mrs. Mary Fitzhugh, June 30, 1698, in Richard Beale Davis, ed., *William Fitzhugh and His Chesapeake World, 1676–1701: The Fitzhugh Letters and Other Documents* (Chapel Hill, University of North Carolina Press, 1963), p. 358.

13. Richard and Elizabeth Ambler to Edward and John Ambler, Aug. 1, 1748, May 20, 1749, in Lucille Griffith, ed., "English Education for Virginia Youth: Some Eighteenth-Century Ambler Family Letters," *Virginia Magazine of History and Biography*, 69 (January 1961):14–16.

14. "The Autobiography of the Reverend Devereux Jarratt," *William and Mary Quarterly*, 3rd. Ser., 9 (July 1952): 361.

15. Kulikoff, *Tobacco and Slaves*, pp. 205–209, 241–242; Natalie Zemon Davis, "Ghosts, Kin and Progeny: Some Features of Family Life in Early Modern France," *Daedalus*, 106 (Winter 1977):92–96.

16. Kulikoff, *Tobacco and Slaves*, pp. 249–253.

17. Daniel Blake Smith, *Inside the Great House: Planter Family Life in Eighteenth-Century Chesapeake Society* (Ithaca, New York, Cornell University Press, 1980), pp. 55–81.

18. "The Diary of M. Ambler, 1770," *Virginia Magazine of History and Biography*, 45 (April 1937):170.

19. Smith, *Inside the Great House*, pp. 88–98; Kulikoff, *Tobacco and Slaves*, p. 151.

20. Russell R. Menard, "Immigrants and Their Increase: The Process of Population Growth in Early Colonial Maryland," in Aubrey C. Land, Lois Green Carr, and Edward C. Papenfuse, eds., *Law, Society and Politics in Early Maryland* (Baltimore, The Johns Hopkins University Press, 1977), pp. 88–110; Morgan, *American Slavery, American Freedom*, pp. 395–423; Kulikoff, *Tobacco and Slaves*, pp. 241–380.

21. Mary Beth Norton, *Liberty's Daughters: The Revolutionary Experience of American Women, 1750–1800* (Boston, Little, Brown and Company, 1980), pp. 27–29, 35–39; Carr and Walsh, "The Planter's Wife"; Joan Hoff Wilson, "The Illusion of Change: Women and the American Revolution," in Alfred F. Young, ed., *The American Revolution: Explorations in the History of American Radicalism* (Dekalb, Northern Illinois University Press, 1976), pp. 389, 393–394, 416–417, 430–431.

22. Charles S. Sydnor, *Gentlemen Freeholders: Political Practices in Washington's Virginia* (Chapel Hill, University of North Carolina Press, 1952); David W. Jordan, "Political Stability and the Emergence of a Native Elite in Maryland," in Tate and Ammerman, eds., *The Chesapeake in the Seventeenth Century*, pp. 243–273.

23. Rhys Issac, *The Transformation of Virginia, 1740–1790* (Chapel Hill, University of North Carolina Press, 1982), pp. 38, 70–71, 78–79, 305.

24. Robert M. Weir, "Rebelliousness: Personality Development and the American Revolution in the Southern Colonies," in Jeffrey J. Crow and Larry E. Tise,

eds., *The Southern Experience in the American Revolution* (Chapel Hill, University of North Carolina Press, 1978), pp. 25–54.

25. Jan Lewis, *The Pursuit of Happiness: Family and Values of Jefferson's Virginia* (New York, Cambridge University Press, 1983), pp. 1–39.

26. Michael Zuckerman, "William Byrd's Family," *Perspectives in American History*, 12 (1979):255–311.

27. Smith, *Inside the Great House*, pp. 163–164, 166–168.

28. Bernard Bailyn, *The Peopling of British North America: An Introduction* (New York, Alfred A. Knopf, 1986), pp. 114, 131.

29. Thomas Jefferson, *Notes on the State of Virginia*, ed. William Peden (Chapel Hill, University of North Carolina Press, 1955), p. 162.

Notes to THREE PLANTERS AND THEIR SLAVES
by Philip Morgan

Mr. Morgan would like to acknowledge the constructive and astute comments offered on earlier drafts of this essay by Robert Middlekauff, Eugene D. Genovese, and members of the Institute of Early American History and Culture colloquium.

1. Gordon J. Schochet, *Patriarchalism in Political Thought: The Authoritarian Family and Political Speculation in Attitudes Especially in Seventeenth-Century England* (New York, Basic Books, 1975); Peter Laslett, *The World We Have Lost* (London, Methuen, 1965), pp. 3–4, 21, 48.

2. Lawrence Stone, *The Family, Sex and Marriage in England 1500–1800* (New York, Harper & Row, 1977); Randolph Trumbach, *The Rise of the Egalitarian Family: Aristocratic Kinship and Domestic Relations in Eighteenth-Century England* (New York, Academic Press, 1978). Both these authors stress marked change by the eighteenth century, but the evidence is primarily for English upper class groups. For somewhat more laggard developments out on the margins, see Daniel Blake Smith, *Inside the Great House: Planter Family Life in Eighteenth-Century Chesapeake Society* (Ithaca, New York, Cornell University Press, 1980); Jan Lewis, *The Pursuit of Happiness: Family and Values in Jefferson's Virginia* (New York, Cambridge University Press, 1983); Jay Fliegelman, *Prodigals and Pilgrims: The American Revolution against Patriarchal Authority, 1750–1800* (New York, Cambridge University Press, 1982); Allan Kulikoff, *Tobacco and Slaves: The Development of Southern Cultures in the Chesapeake, 1680–1800* (Chapel Hill, University of North Carolina Press, 1986), pp. 7–8, 165–204; and Shomer Zwelling, "The Transformation of Robert Carter III: From Colonial Patriarch to Christian Pilgrim" (unpublished paper). These authors, need it be said, disagree on timing, with Kulikoff basically arguing for continuities in patriarchalism over the century and the others, to a greater or lesser degree, arguing for changes. Cf. a fine essay, but one that exaggerates change and pays insufficient attention to the plantation colonies, Edwin G. Burrows and Michael Wallace, "The American Revolution: The Ideology and Psychology of National Liberation," *Perspectives in American History*, 6 (1972):167–308. For an unpersuasive account of an early eighteenth-century Virginian's supposed "transformation" toward his slaves, see Kenneth A. Lockridge, *The Diary, and Life, of William Byrd II of Virginia, 1674–1744* (Chapel Hill, University of North Carolina Press, 1987).

3. William Darrell, *The Gentleman Instructed* (London, 1727), Pt. i., 87, cited in J. Jean Hecht, *The Domestic Servant Class in Eighteenth Century England*

(London, Routledge & Kegan Paul, 1956), p. 75; William Fleetwood, *The Relative Duties of Parents and Children, Husbands and Wives, Masters and Servants, Consider'd in Sixteen Sermons: With Three More Upon the Case of Self-Murther* (London, C. Harper, 1705), p. 385. See also Ann Kussmaul, *Servants in Husbandry in Early Modern England* (Cambridge, Cambridge University Press, 1981).

4. *Oxford English Dictionary*, "family"; Gerald W. Mullin, *Flight and Rebellion: Slave Resistance in Eighteenth-Century Virginia* (New York, Oxford University Press, 1972), p. 19 and passim.

5. Hecht, *Domestic Servant Class*, pp. 71–124; Kussmaul, *Servants in Husbandry*, pp. 31–69.

6. Newbell Niles Puckett, "Names of American Negro Slaves," in George P. Murdock, ed., *Studies in the Science of Society* (New Haven, Yale University Press, 1937), pp. 478–481; Darrett B. Rutman and Anita H. Rutman, *A Place in Time: Explicatus* (New York, W.W. Norton, 1984), p. 101.

7. Frederick Cooper, *Plantation Slavery on the East Coast of Africa* (New Haven, Yale University Press, 1977), p. 2 and passim. I think James Oakes has oversimplified matters in his depiction of a deep and growing tension between paternalism and liberalism, between an organic social order and free market commercialism, between the familial and proprietorial view of slaves. For him, masters regarded slaves primarily as property, as little more than "disembodied abstractions." James Oakes, *The Ruling Race: A History of American Slaveholders* (New York, Alfred A. Knopf, 1982), pp. xiv, 27, passim.

8. Rhys Isaac, *The Transformation of Virginia, 1740–1790* (Chapel Hill, University of North Carolina Press, 1982), pp. 309, 320. By far the best study of nineteenth-century paternalism and of slave life, in general, is Eugene D. Genovese, *Roll, Jordan, Roll: The World the Slaves Made* (New York, Pantheon, 1974). See page 6 of this work for the suggestion that paternalism arose ca. 1750. On the role of sentiment in nineteenth-century paternalistic thinking, see George B. Forgie, *Patricide in the House Divided: A Psychological Interpretation of Lincoln and His Age* (New York, W.W. Norton, 1979). For excellent discussions of paternalism in other contexts, see David Roberts, *Paternalism in Early Victorian England* (New Brunswick, New Jersey Rutgers University Press, 1979) and, more particularly, the sophisticated work of Patrick Joyce, *Work, Society, and Politics: The Culture of the Factory in Later Victorian England* (Brighton, England, Harvester Press, 1980). For recent definitions of patriarchy and paternalism, somewhat more general than those implied here, see Gerda Lerner, *The Creation of Patriarchy* (New York, Oxford University Press, 1986), pp. 238–240.

9. All my information on Landon Carter derives, unless otherwise stated, from Jack P. Greene, ed., *The Diary of Landon Carter of Sabine Hall, 1752–1778*, 2 vols. (Charlottesville, University Press of Virginia, 1965) [since the volumes are paginated consecutively, I will just refer to page numbers]; inventory of the estate of Landon Carter, Esq, Feb. 1779, Carter Family Papers, College of William and Mary. In addition to the 401 slaves Carter owned at his death, he had already deeded at least 56 slaves to his sons: will of Landon Carter, Feb. 12, 1779, *Virginia Magazine of History and Biography*, 29 (July 1921):361. It is extremely difficult to discover how many quarters Carter operated at any one time. He mentions about 16 in Richmond County alone over the course of the diary (apart from the Fork, Home, and Mangorike quarters, there are Hickory Thicket, Island, Lansdowne, Locust Point, Oliver's Branch, and Riverside, as well as others named for overseers or slaves). In other counties he notes Acquia and Park quarters in Stafford; Bloughpoint and unnamed others (probably 2 more) in Northumberland; Bull

Run in Loudoun; Ring's Neck and Rippon Hall in York; and unnamed others in Fauquier, King and Queen, Lancaster, and Prince William. My estimate is therefore distinctly conservative.

10. Greene, ed., *Landon Carter Diary*, index by name of slave.

11. The 10 slaves were in descending order: Nassau, Manuel, Talbot, Nat, Toney, George, Gardiner Johnny, Fork Jammy, Mulatto Betty, and Guy. Of the slaves identifiable by sex and age, Carter named 96 men, 57 women, 19 boys, and 8 girls in his diary. In 1773 Landon Carter reported 36 male and 33 female tithables for Lunenburg Parish, Richmond County. I calculate that he mentions all but one of these slave men, but only three-quarters of the women in his diary. Applying the same analysis to the inventory of 1779 (which includes children, of course), I estimate that his diary mentions 60% of the males and 50% of the females in Richmond County (out of a total of 97 males and 84 females, with 6 undecipherable). The reporting rate drops dramatically for the other counties: 4 males and 1 female in Northumberland County (out of 33 males and 39 females, with 2 undecipherable), 1 slave man in York County (out of 13 males and 18 females), and no slaves from Prince William and Loudoun Counties (23 males, 30 females, and 3 children), or from Stafford (17 males and 16 females), or from King and Queen, Westmoreland, and Fauquier counties (14 males, 4 females, and 1 child). Tithable list, 1773, is in Carter Family Papers, Sabine Hall Collection, University of Virginia, microfilm.

12. Greene, ed., *Landon Carter Diary*, pp. 797, 202, 254, 353, 377–378, 411, 417, 470, 505, 520–521, 526, 554–555, 568, 572, 577, 580, 595–596, 622, 627–629, 635–636, 667, 758, 765, 769, 776, 779, 781, 794, 811, 829, 841–842, 866, 903, 946–947, 952, 993, 996, 1111, 1145.

13. Ibid., pp. 1036, 628, 651, 665, 793, 583.

14. Ibid., pp. 940, 953. See also pp. 347, 363, 373, 411, 490–492, 527, 775–776, 778, 782, 847, 947, 952, 1088, 1096, 1145.

15. Ibid., p. 778.

16. Landon Carter, *Virginia Gazette* (Rind), Mar. 3, 1768, as cited in Mullin, *Flight and Rebellion*, p. 78. In this advertisement, Carter offered wages to any "young man with a good disposition, that can shave and bleed well." Characteristically, Carter believed that such a man would learn much from such a knowledgeable master. Presumably, Carter could find no taker.

17. Greene, ed., *Landon Carter Diary*, pp. 492, 778.

18. Ibid., p. 941.

19. Ibid., pp. 953, 1088, 1096, 1145. Mullin argues that Nassau ran off to the British in 1777. If he did, he was back in Carter's service by 1778. However, he did run off on the very last day Carter mentions him, i.e., Aug. 16, 1778. But this was another of Nassau's bouts of absenteeism (for others see ibid., pp. 783–784, 1128), since he is listed in Carter's inventory.

20. Ibid., pp. 396, 449, 456, 470, 817, 510, 545, 486. Carter's ambivalence toward Manuel could be illustrated with many of his skilled slaves, such as carpenter Toney or foreman/artisan Jamy of Fork quarter, or indeed with those who had the same sort of responsibilities as Manuel, i.e., Peter and Talbot.

21. Ibid., pp. 296, 367–368, 396–397, 442, 495, 504, 536, 541, 611, 724.

22. Ibid., pp. 396–397 and 1051–1052, 1109–1110; Peter Charles Hoffer, ed., *Criminal Proceedings in Colonial Virginia: [Records of] Fines, Examination of Criminals, Trials of Slaves, etc., from March 1710 [1711] to [1754] [Richmond County, Virginia]* (Athens, University of Georgia Press, 1984), pp. 236–238. Manuel was not the only slave to gain from Carter's "protection" when due

process intervened: see Greene, ed., *Landon Carter Diary*, p. 1110. See also Gwenda Morgan, "Hegemony of the Law: Richmond County, 1692–1776," Ph.D. Dissertation, The Johns Hopkins University, 1980, pp. 134–135.

23. David Hackett Fischer, *Growing Old in America*, expanded edition (New York, Oxford University Press, 1978), especially pp. 26–76; Greene, ed., *Landon Carter Diary*, pp. 840–841, 834, 836. See also pp. 301, 303, 547, 556, 567, 574–575. Carter expected gratitude from his elderly slaves, as witness his complaint, "[e]ven the most aged, whilst their lives are made most pleasant to them, are the most ungratefully neglectful," ibid., p. 295.

24. Ibid., pp. 487, 454–455. Sukey was Manuel's wife. As another example of an old slave who made a distinct impression on Landon Carter, consider his recollections about his father's slave, Old Nassau, the only carter his father had employed, ibid., p. 1038. We know from other evidence that this Nassau was an important slave and possessed a canoe: see Robert "King" Carter diary, Jan. 13, 1725, microfilm, Colonial Williamsburg.

25. Runaways can be followed in the index; the outlaws were Simon, Guy, Robin, and Nassau; for Johnny and George, see Greene, ed., *Landon Carter Diary*, pp. 589 and 218. Landon Carter placed at least two runaway advertisements in local newspapers. It is instructive that his diary records the departure of Phil, who ran away from Sabine Hall [Carter was proved correct in his assumption that Phil had not run off to the British: *VaG* (Purdie), Apr. 5, 1776 and Greene, ed., *Landon Carter Diary*, p. 1010], but is silent about his other advertised runaway, a 21 or 22 year old man, who absented himself in Oct. 1774 from Carter's Fauquier County quarter. He went by the name of "Isham, to which he adds sometimes Randolph, at others Allen," *VaG* (Dixon & Hunter), Feb. 25, 1775. A Randolph is listed on Carter's Fauquier quarter in 1779.

26. Whippings can be traced in the index under slave punishment; for Guy, see Greene, ed., *Landon Carter Diary*, p. 371. Carter ordered his female cowkeeper Sicely to be "severely slashed" in 1772: ibid., p. 672.

27. Ibid., pp. 196, 357, 493, 495, 519, 616. On slave tasks throughout the year, almost any page of the diary is relevant.

28. Ibid., pp. 422; 306, 428, 430, 451, 453, 517, 681; 430, 451, 577, 612.

29. Ibid., pp. 1137–1138, 305, 567.

30. Ibid., pp. 174, 588. See also pp. 127, 159, 384, 428, 524, 536, 554, 939, 1128.

31. Ibid., p. 425. See also pp. 308, 375–376, 397, 423, 431, 465.

32. For some examples, see ibid., pp. 147, 177, 295, 300, 302, 355, 386, 408, 426, 430, 451, 508, 536, 568, 579, 678–679, 681, 755, 834, 864.

33. Ibid., pp. 396, 399, 429, 465–466, 494, 496, 691, 952.

34. Ibid., pp. 451, 274. See also pp. 158, 200, 253, 374–375, 426, 534.

35. Ibid., pp. 751. Emphasis mine.

36. Ibid., pp. 130–131. Apart from work, illness is the most frequent subject when Carter speaks of his slaves. See index.

37. Ibid., pp. 785, 348–349. On two occasions, Carter shared his private passion for medical matters with a wider public: *VaG* (Purdie & Dixon), Dec. 3, 1772 and ibid. (Rind), Apr. 14, 1774.

38. Greene, ed., *Landon Carter Diary* pp. 648, 649–650, 651–654, 656, 768, 942–943, 990, 993–998. Nor did other slaves unquestioningly accept Carter's role as doctor, see pp. 742, 865.

39. Ibid., pp. 1051–2, 1109–1110.

40. Ibid., pp. 632–633, 635, 631, 554–556, 651, 664.

41. Ibid., p. 1064.

42. Ibid., pp. 554–555, 609–610. See also pp. 379 and 1059 for other family traits.

43. Manuel's known children include Billy, Harry, Peg, Sarah and Will. For the more dramatic incidents, see *ibid.*, pp. 372, 517, 777, 1012, 1051–1052, 1110. Carter also understood that domination and resistance occurred within slave families: Pantico beat his wife Nelly, who was of such a "firy" temper that no husband would stay with her long [*ibid.*, pp. 383, 865].

44. For Nat and Talbot drinking, see *ibid.*, pp. 373, 526, 927; foreman George, Joe, and carpenters Ralph and Toney all passed their names on to one of their sons. Nassau seems to have engaged in the necronymic naming practice of the times: in 1757 his son Nat died [*ibid.*, p. 159], but in 1770 he had obviously passed on the name to another son [*ibid.*, pp. 345, 348–349, 373, and *passim.*].

45. Ibid., p. 218.

46. Ibid., pp. 289–292. See Isaac, *Transformation of Virginia*, pp. 329–341 for an extended analysis of this incident.

47. Greene, ed., *Landon Carter Diary*, pp. 1124, 666.

48. Ibid., pp. 291, 397, 443, 544, 547. See also p. 362.

49. Ibid., pp. 371–372. See also p. 496.

50. Ibid., pp. 760, 762. For another grandparent-grandchild relationship, see p. 771.

51. Ibid., pp. 589, 636, 778, 941. For a similar argument to the one here, see Rhys Isaac, "Communication and Control: Authority Metaphors and Power Contests on Colonel Landon Carter's Virginia Plantation, 1752–1778," in Sean Wilentz, ed., *Rites of Power: Symbolism, Ritual, and Politics Since the Middle Ages* (Philadelphia, University of Pennsylvania Press, 1985), pp. 275–302.

52. This account of Laurens's plantations (and his relationship with his slaves) rests on Philip Hamer, George C. Rogers, David Chestnut *et al.*, eds., *The Papers of Henry Laurens*, 10 vols. to date (Columbia, University of South Carolina Press, 1965–1985); South Carolina Historical Society, Papers of Henry Laurens (microfilm); typescripts of Laurens papers, kindly made available to me by editors of the Laurens Papers at the University of South Carolina, Columbia; David D. Wallace, *The Life of Henry Laurens, With a Sketch of the Life of Lieutenant-Colonel John Laurens* (New York, G.P. Putnam's Sons, 1915); will of Henry Laurens, Nov. 1, 1792, Will Book B (1786–1793), pp. 1152–1158, South Carolina Department of Archives and History, Columbia; account book of Henry Laurens, 1766–1773, College of Charleston.

53. In descending order, they are Scipio, Samuel, Scaramouch, Stepney, and Shrewsbury. Among the slaves who can be differentiated by age and sex, Laurens mentions 119 men, 35 women, 15 boys, and 8 girls. Unfortunately, no listings exist for Laurens's slaves so it is impossible to calculate a rudimentary reporting rate. Still, the dimensions of the difference between this age-sex profile and that mentioned by Landon Carter are abundantly clear. Since an inventory of estate does not exist for Laurens, it is impossible to determine how many slaves he owned at the end of his life; but, in 1790, he reported 298 [U.S. Bureau of the Census, *Heads of Families at the First Census of the United States Taken in the Year 1790: South Carolina* (Washington, D.C., Government Printing Office, 1908), p. 31]. In 1766, his own accounts indicate that he owned 239 and, 12 years later, he seems to have possessed about 260 slaves. Many of these were Africans, so his slave complement probably grew rather slowly from natural increase. Moreover, the Revolutionary war had devastating effects on a number of Laurens's

plantations, which probably depressed growth rates further, even if few of his slaves ran away to the British. On slaves belonging to Laurens who were stolen by, or ran away to, the British, see Henry Laurens to John Owen, Mar. 4, 1784, Laurens typescripts.

54. Hamer *et al.*, eds., *Laurens Papers*, 4:632–633, 664–665; 6:181–182; 7:219, 228. Laurens bought Scipio from the Reverend Samuel Fenner Warren for £320 "some years past," account book, Apr. 1771, p. 377.

55. Hamer *et al.*, eds., *Laurens Papers*, 8:1, 16, 26–27, 156, 286, 335, 342–343, 639, 4, and 47.

56. Ibid., 8:227, 232, 658; 9:316–318, 347.

57. Ibid., 4:661–662; 5:702.

58. Ibid., 7:566; 8:67–68, 96; 10:2–3, 17, 203, 205; account book, Nov. 1772 and Jan. 1773, pp. 493 and 501. Emphasis on *friends* mine.

59. Hamer *et al.*, eds., *Laurens Papers*, 3:203; 7:329. Economic calculation was a primary concern, of course. Laurens's last reference to Cudjo couples a solicitous inquiry about the slave's health and the following statement, "I am paying Wages for him & not certain of his being alive," ibid., 9:262–263.

60. Ibid., 5:120; 6:445–446, 612; 8:399, 635; 9:575–576; account book, Feb. 1772, p. 462; John Lewis Gervais to Henry Laurens, Aug. 17, 1778, Laurens typescripts.

61. Hamer *et al.*, eds., *Laurens Papers*, 4:241, 587–588, 608, 662; 5:46, 62, 77, 94, 101, 378, 380, 70.

62. Ibid., 8:124, 66–67, 73, 172, 505; 9:204, 269, 414, 460, 512; John Lewis Gervais to Henry Laurens, Aug. 17, 1778 and Sept. 9, 1778, Laurens typescripts.

63. Hamer *et al.*, eds., *Laurens Papers*, 4:298–299. For more on Abraham, see ibid., 4:616, 633; 5:3, 11, 16, 67, 70, 379. Laurens had difficulties with many boatmen. See his relations with Amos, George, Mingo, and Scaramouch, for instance.

64. Ibid., 8:618; 4:624; account book, Sept. 26, 1772, p. 491.

65. Hamer *et al.*, eds., *Laurens Papers*, 10:579; 4:503; Henry Laurens to William Bell, Dec. 2, 1786, Laurens Papers, SCHS (mfm). See also Hamer *et al.*, eds., *Laurens Papers*, 3:203, 205; 4:632; 5:61, 144; 8:6; 9:592, 627; John Lewis Gervais to Henry Laurens, Aug. 17, 1778 and Henry Laurens to John Owen, Mar. 4, 1784, Laurens typescripts.

66. Henry Laurens to Edward Rutledge, May 24, 1786, Laurens Papers, SCHS (mfm).

67. Hamer *et al.*, eds., *Laurens Papers*, 10:234; 8:11, 66–67; 9:262.

68. Ibid., 10:162–163.

69. Henry Laurens to Jacob Read, July 16 and Sept. 15, 1785, Laurens Papers, SCHS (mfm).

70. Hamer *et al.*, eds., *Laurens Papers*, 4:666; 5:379; 8:617–618; 9:576, 316–317. Laurens has been portrayed as an opponent of slavery (see Wallace, *Life of Laurens*, pp. 445–454). It is true that he did once say he abhorred slavery, and his son John was certainly a radical critic of the institution. However, although Laurens did not like slavery, he was no idealist. He once spoke of manumitting his slaves, but never attempted to do so. Like many other slaveowners, his misgivings about slavery were offset by social custom, by the ease and profits to be derived from it, and by the belief that its victims were unfit for freedom.

71. Hamer *et al.*, eds., *Laurens Papers*, 4:596.

72. Wallace, *Life of Laurens*, p. 425; Henry Laurens to John Laurens, Aug. 1, 1776, Charleston Library Society Miscellaneous Mss; Henry Laurens to William Bell, Apr. 25, 1785, Laurens Papers, SCHS (mfm).

73. Henry Laurens to William Manning, Dec. 17, 1774, Laurens typescripts.

74. Hamer et al., eds., Laurens Papers, 5:227; 4:633; 8:617; 3:205.

75. Ibid., 4:633, 665–666; 5:171; 8:73.

76. Laurens's first runaway whom he sells is mentioned ibid., 4:645. For other sales later in life, see John Lewis Gervais to Henry Laurens, Aug. 17, 1778, Laurens typescripts.

77. Hamer et al., eds., Laurens Papers, 5:200; 6:149–150 and 7:192; 5:227 and 6:438. Apparently, Carter used cowskins on his plantations: see Greene, ed., Landon Carter Diary, p. 495.

78. Hamer et al., eds., Laurens Papers, 4:148, 625; 5:62.

79. Ibid., 3:203; 4:319; account book, Apr. 1771, p. 377. The size of a name pool is a good indicator of the scale of planter interference in the naming of slaves. The name pool among Carter's slaves is surprisingly small, which could hardly have been the design of the master. Thus, of the 165 Carter slaves mentioned, 106 or 64% shared a name with another slave (there were, for instance, 8 Toms, 7 Marys, 6 Sarahs, and 6 Bettys). Carter had to rely on modifiers (quarter names, for instance) to differentiate among his slaves. Laurens's slaves, on the other hand, reveal a much larger pool, confirming the evidence of far greater intrusion from the master. Of 147 slaves belonging to Laurens, only 35 or 24% shared the same name (there were 5 Jacks, 3 Harrys, and 3 Peters).

80. Ibid., 4:595–596.

81. Ibid., 4:579; 5:123, 485; account book, Sept. 1768, p. 184.

82. Hamer et al., eds., Laurens Papers, 8:239; 5:370.

83. Ibid., 9:575–576, 204; John Lewis Gervais to Henry Laurens, Feb. 12, 1784, Laurens typescripts; Hamer et al., eds., Laurens Papers, 8:98–99; 9:262; 5:125.

84. Ibid., 8:288, 291; 7:443.

85. Ibid., 5:175; 8:66–67. For another slave well versed in indigo cultivation, see 5:125; for drivers, see 5:574, 592.

86. Ibid., 1:242; 4:148; 9:109, 188–189; 5:123.

87. Ibid., 8:128; 9:268; 8:96; 5:702; 8:348. Landon Carter mentions only one slave practice that seems African in origin, i.e., head-carrying. See Greene, ed., Landon Carter Diary, pp. 554, 897.

88. Hamer et al., eds., Laurens Papers, 4:616; 5:20, 41; account book, Mar. 1769, p. 217, Mar. 1773, p. 508. See also Hamer et al., eds., Laurens Papers, 5:93. For independent slave production and exchanges with whites on Carter's plantations—on a much smaller scale, in my opinion—see Greene, ed., Landon Carter Diary, pp. 390, 396, 483–484, 602, 871, 988, 1095–1096.

89. Hamer et al., eds., Laurens Papers, 4:656, 5:99–100.

90. This account of Thomas Thistlewood is based on my reading of his diaries, 1748–1786, Monson MSS 31/1–37, and related materials in Lincolnshire County Record Office, Lincoln, England. I am grateful to Lord and Lady Monson for allowing me to quote from these documents. My analysis of these diaries has been greatly aided by a grant from the Research Program of the National Endowment for the Humanities [RT-20566] and by the expert assistance of Barbara Morgan. For other brief uses of the diary, see Owen A. Sherrard, Freedom From Fear: The Slave and His Emancipation (New York, St. Martin's Press, 1961), pp. 85–97; J. R. Ward, "A Planter and His Slaves in Eighteenth-Century Jamaica," in T. C. Smout, ed., The Search for Wealth and Stability: Essays in Economic and Social History Presented to M. W. Flinn (London, Macmillan, 1979), pp. 1–21; Michael Craton, Testing the Chains: Resistance to Slavery in the British West Indies (Ithaca, New York, Cornell University Press, 1982), pp. 38–43, 48–49, 92–93, 133–135; Richard S. Dunn, "Servants and Slaves: The Recruitment and Employment of Labor," in

Jack P. Greene and J. R. Pole, eds., *Colonial British America: Essays in the New History of the Early Modern Era* (Baltimore, The Johns Hopkins University Press, 1984), pp. 173–174. Douglas Hall, professor emeritus of the University of West Indies, Mona, is writing a biography of Thistlewood. I plan to write a monograph exploring Thistlewood's world.

91. Diary, Jan. 8, 1751, 31/2/5. Thistlewood mentions 39 men, 28 women, 3 boys, and 3 girls in 1750; 93 men, 53 women, 8 boys, and no girls in 1752. Apparently, children are infrequently mentioned. It is interesting that the male-female ratios derived from these figures are much more favorable than those reported by Laurens.

92. I am producing an analytical index of all the entries in the diary, which will be available on computer tape. The episodes in this paragraph can be easily followed under the entry "sexual encounters."

93. Ditto, under "Phibbah," in 1753.

94. Ditto, under "Phibbah," in 1757 and for subsequent years.

95. Ditto, under "Sharper, old" from 1750 on.

96. Ditto, under "Quashe, Mason" for 1752. Many other skilled slaves filled Thistlewood with equally ambivalent feelings.

97. Ditto, under entries such as "music," "folk tales," "duppies," and "dogs."

98. Ditto, under "gifts," "clothing," "health," etc.

99. Ditto, under "punishment" and individual slave names for number of lashes; also see "runaways."

100. All these examples are drawn from the diaries for 1750 and 1751.

101. See entries such as "canes, cutting of," "canes, transporting of," or "boiling house" in the index to the diary in 1752.

102. Ditto, under "Negroes," "holidays," "corn," and "plantains."

103. Ditto, under "Will, mulatto, slave" in the year 1758.

104. Robert Filmer, *Patriarcha and Other Political Works.* ed. Peter Laslett (Oxford, Basil Blackwell, 1949), pp. 63, 99.

105. Greene, ed., *Landon Carter Diary*, p. 1149; Hamer *et al.*, eds., *Laurens Papers*, 2:123; 4:602; 5:125.

106. Greene, ed., *Landon Carter Diary*, p. 845; Henry Laurens to Moses Young, Feb. 8 and June 14, 1787, Laurens Papers, SCHS (mfm). For two cases of slaves seemingly identifying with their master's territorial claim, see Greene, ed., *Landon Carter Diary*, pp. 397–398, 1142.

107. See entry for "Roger, mason, slave."

108. For an interesting essay that implicitly recognizes the difference between paternalism and patriarchalism, but without doing the distinction full justice, see Paul Conner, "Patriarchy: Old World and New," *American Quarterly*, 17 (Spring 1965):48–62, especially pp. 54–55 for Fitzhugh quotes. Similarly, see Michael P. Johnson, "Planters and Patriarchy: Charleston, 1800–1860," *Journal of Southern History*, 46 (February 1980):45–72. Bernard Bailyn has recently noted that in Anglo-American slave societies in the eighteenth century, "an accommodation was somehow made between brutality and progressive refinement," or between "despotism" and "domestic gentility," *The Peopling of British North America: An Introduction* (New York, Alfred A. Knopf, 1986), pp. 118, 120.

109. Mathew Gregory Lewis, *Journal of a West-India Proprietor, kept during a residence in the Island of Jamaica* (London, J. Murray, 1834); Maria Nugent, *Lady Nugent's Journal, Jamaica One Hundred Years Ago*, ed. Frank Cundall (London, A. & C. Black, 1907).

110. Orlando Patterson, *Slavery and Social Death: A Comparative Study* (Cambridge, Harvard University Press, 1982), p. 207.

111. For one author who glimpsed this irony, but who had the cruel misfortune not to be able to develop it, see Willie Lee Rose, *Slavery and Freedom*, ed. William W. Freehling, expanded edition (New York, Oxford University Press, 1982), especially pp. 18–36. I do not, however, fully accept Professor Rose's characterization of eighteenth-century planters.

Notes to THE AFRICANIZATION OF THE LOWCOUNTRY LABOR FORCE
by Russell R. Menard

Earlier versions of this paper were presented to the Slavery Seminar of the W.E.B. Dubois Institute for Afro-American Research at Harvard University, the Economic History Workshop of Indiana University, and the Social History Workshop of the University of Minnesota. Research support was provided by the Graduate School of the University of Minnesota. Thanks are due to Susan Cahn and Deborah Kitchen who served as research assistants, and, especially, to Stuart Schwartz for a decade of conversation on slavery in the Americas.

1. For a survey of recent work on the Carolina Lowcountry see John J. Mc-Cusker and Russell R. Menard, *The Economy of British America, 1607–1789* (Chapel Hill, University of North Carolina Press, 1985), pp. 169–188.

2. Samuel Dyssli to his mother, brothers and friends in Switzerland, Dec. 3, 1737, *South Carolina Historical and Geneological Magazine*, 23 (July 1922): 90, as quoted in Peter H. Wood, "'More Like a Negro Country': Demographic Patterns in Colonial South Carolina, 1700–1740," in Stanley L. Engerman and Eugene D. Genovese, eds., *Race and Slavery in the Western Hemisphere: Quantitative Studies* (Princeton, Princeton University Press, 1975), pp. 131–132.

3. For the population in 1708, see below, Table 2. On Stono see Peter H. Wood, *Black Majority: Negroes in Colonial South Carolina from 1670 through the Stono Rebellion* (New York, Alfred A. Knopf, 1974), pp. 308–326. On the depression of the 1740s see Stuart O. Stumpf, "Implications of King George's War for the Charleston Mercantile Community," *South Carolina Historical and Geneological Magazine*, 77 (July 1976): 161–188. For Charleston's black population see Philip D. Morgan, "Black Life in Eighteenth-Century Charleston," *Perspectives in American History*, N.S., 1 (1984):188. For slavery in the backcountry see Robert L. Meriwether, *The Expansion of South Carolina, 1729–1765* (Kingsport, Tennessee, Southern Publishers, Inc., 1940). On the black percentage of the population in the Lowcountry plantation district see, for example, George D. Terry, "'Champaign Country': A Social History of an Eighteenth Century Lowcountry Parish in South Carolina, St. Johns Berkeley County," Ph.D. Dissertation, University of South Carolina, 1981, p. 116.

4. The tax list is printed in Philip D. Morgan, ed., "A Profile of a Mid-Eighteenth Century South Carolina Parish: The Tax Return of St. James', Goose Greek," *South Carolina Historical and Geneological Magazine*, 81 (January 1980):51–65.

5. James F. Shepherd and Gary M. Walton, "Economic Change After the American Revolution: Pre- and Post-War Comparisons of Maritime Shipping and Trade," *Explorations in Economic History*, 13 (October 1976):397–422.

6. William G. Bentley, "Wealth Distribution in Colonial South Carolina," Ph.D. Dissertation, Georgia State University, 1977, pp. 82, 84, 104; Alice Hanson Jones, *American Colonial Wealth: Documents and Methods* (New York, Arno Press, 1977), vol. 3, pp. 2165–2167; Jones, *Wealth of a Nation to Be: The American*

Colonies on the Eve of the Revolution (New York, Columbia University Press, 1980), pp. 171, 179, 379.

7. Robert M. Weir, *Colonial South Carolina: A History* (Millwood, New York, KTO Press, 1983), p. 263; "Dr. Milligin-Johnston's Additions' to His Pamphlet," in Chapman J. Milling, ed., *Colonial South Carolina: Two Contemporary Descriptions* (Columbia, University of South Carolina Press, 1951), p. 109.

8. Bentley, "Wealth Distribution in Colonial South Carolina," pp. 82, 84, 104; Morgan, "Profile of a South Carolina Parish"; Terry, "'Champaign Country,'" pp. 148–149; Jackson T. Main, *The Social Structure of Revolutionary America* (Princeton, Princeton University Press, 1965), pp. 57–61; Weir, *Colonial South Carolina*, pp. 213-218; and Richard Waterhouse, "South Carolina's Colonial Elite: A Study in the Social Structure and Political Culture of a Southern Colony, 1670–1760," Ph.D. Dissertation, The Johns Hopkins University, 1973.

9. I plan to address this issue in detail later. For a preliminary statement see Russell R. Menard, "Slavery, Economic Growth, and Revolutionary Ideology in the Carolina Lowcountry," in Ronald Hoffman, John J. McCusker, Russell R. Menard, and Peter J. Albert, eds., *The Economy of Early America: The Revolutionary Period, 1763–1790* (Charlottesville, University of Virginia Press, forthcoming).

10. Richard S. Dunn, *Sugar and Slaves: The Rise of the Planter Class in the English West Indies, 1624-1713* (Chapel Hill, University of North Carolina Press, 1972).

11. Of the large literature on the Chesapeake gentry see especially Edmund S. Morgan, *American Slavery, American Freedom: The Ordeal of Colonial Virginia* (New York, W. W. Norton, 1975), and Allan Kulikoff, *Tobacco and Slaves: The Development of Southern Cultures in the Chesapeake, 1680–1800* (Chapel Hill, University of North Carolina Press, 1986).

12. McCusker and Menard, *Economy of British America*, pp. 91–208, surveys the literature with an eye to identifying regional variations.

13. David Brion Davis, *Slavery and Human Progress* (New York, Oxford University Press, 1984), p. 52.

14. Wood, *Black Majority*, p. 37.

15. Wood, *Black Majority*, pp. 13–91, is the best introduction to the issues.

16. Governor and Council of Carolina to the Council of Trade and Plantations, Sept. 17, 1709, CO 5/1264, 82, Public Records Office, London.

17. The composition of the Lowcountry work force in the 1730s is discussed in more detail below.

18. A note of caution is in order here. The figures reported in Table 3 do not provide a guide to the changing volume of migration: there are simply too many omissions, duplications, and gaps, while the record keeping was neither consistent nor careful. However, there seems no reason to doubt that they accurately reflect the changing composition of the migrant group. On the use of headright records as a measure of migration see McCusker and Menard, *Economy of British America*, pp. 222–223, and the works cited there.

19. A third transition centered on the rise of a native-born Afro-American slave population also began in this period, albeit slowly and tentatively, but was still far from complete at the outbreak of the Revolution. It is beyond the scope of this essay, although I plan to address it shortly. For an introduction to the issue see Philip David Morgan, "The Development of Slave Culture in Eighteenth Century Plantation America," Ph.D. Dissertation, University College, London, 1977.

20. The analysis that follows is informed by the approach to colonial labor

markets taken in Henry A. Gemery and Jan S. Hogendorn, "The Atlantic Slave Trade: A Tentative Economic Model," *Journal of African History*, 15 (1974):223–246, and David W. Galenson, *White Servitude in Colonial America: An Economic Analysis* (New York, Cambridge University Press, 1981), especially pp. 141–149.

21. Robert Southwell to Lord Ashley, Aug. 31, 1669, South Carolina Historical Society *Collections*, 5 (1897): 152–153.

22. Henry A. Gemery, "Emigration from the British Isles to the New World: Inferences from Colonial Populations," *Research in Economic History*, 5 (1980): 179–231.

23. Joseph West to Lord Ashley, Sept.1670, South Carolina Historical Society *Collections*, 5 (1897): 203; Joel Gascoyne, *A True Description of Carolina* (London, 1682), pp. 1–2.

24. *South Carolina Historical and Geneological Magazine*, 30 (April 1929):72–73; "A Contemporary View of Carolina in 1680," *South Carolina Historical and Geneological Magazine*, 55 (July 1954):157; Thomas Ashe, *Carolina, or a Description of the Present State of that Country* (London, 1682), in Alexander S. Salley, Jr., ed., *Narratives of Early Carolina, 1650–1708* (New York, Scribner, 1911), p. 141; Lords Proprietors of Carolina to Governor Sir Richard Kyrle, June 3, 1684, in *Records in the British Public Record Office relating to South Carolina, 1663–1684* (Atlanta, 1928), vol. 1, p. 293. There are no precise data on mortality in early South Carolina, although evidence gathered by Aaron Shatzman suggests very high death rates among new arrivals (only 102 of 241 servants in the colony during the 1670s appeared in the records as free settlers) followed by mortality levels similar to those reported for immigrants to the Chesapeake region. Aaron M. Shatzman, "Servants into Planters: The Origins of an American Image: Land Acquisition and Status in Seventeenth-Century South Carolina," Ph.D. Dissertation, Stanford University, 1981, pp. 137–138. See also H. Roy Merrens and George D. Terry, "Dying in Paradise: Malaria, Mortality, and the Perceptual Environment in Colonial South Carolina," *Journal of Southern History*, 50 (November 1984):533–550, and Peter Coclanis, "Death in Early Charleston: An Estimate of the Crude Death Rate for the White Population of Charleston," *South Carolina Historical and Geneological Magazine*, 85 (October 1984):280–291.

25. Galenson, *White Servitude*, pp. 220–221, 224–225. On the role of merchants in the recruiting process see Bernard Bailyn, *Voyagers to the West: A Passage in the Peopling of America on the Eve of the Revolution* (New York, Alfred A. Knopf, 1986), pp. 296–323.

26. On the immigration from Barbados to South Carolina see Richard S. Dunn, "The English Sugar Islands and the Founding of South Carolina," *South Carolina Historical and Geneological Magazine*, 72 (April 1971):81–93; St. Julien Ravenel Childs, "The First South Carolinians," *ibid.*, 71 (April 1970):101–108; Wood, *Black Majority*, pp. 3–34; Adelaide Berta Helwig, "The Early History of Barbados and her Influence upon the Development of South Carolina," Ph.D. Dissertation, University of California, Berkeley, 1930; and Richard Waterhouse, "England, the Caribbean, and the Settlement of Carolina," *Journal of American Studies*, 9 (December 1975):259–281. For the proportion of servants from Barbados see Shatzman, "Servant into Planter," p. 95.

27. On passage costs from Barbados to Carolina see Records of the Secretary of the Province, 1675–1695, p. 128, South Carolina Department of Archives and History. The cost of passage from England to Carolina at this time was £6 sterling. Records of the Secretary, 1694–1703, p. 33. For the short terms of servants from Barbados see Warren B. Smith, *White Servitude in Colonial South Carolina*

(Columbia, University of South Carolina Press, 1961), p. 7. For short terms among English servants see Wood, *Black Majority*, pp.40–41.

28. West to Ashley, March 21, 1671, South Carolina Historical Society *Collections*, 5 (1897):299.

29. Thomas Cooper and David J. McCord, eds., *The Statutes at Large of South Carolina* (Columbia, A. S. Johnston, 1836–1841), vol. 2, pp. 153–156.

30. "An Interview with James Freeman, 1712," quoted in Harry Roy Merrens, *The Colonial South Carolina Scene: Contemporary Views, 1697–1774*, (Columbia, University of South Carolina Press, 1977), p. 51. See also Samuel Wilson, *An Account of the Province of Carolina, in America* (London, 1682), in Salley, ed., *Narratives*, p. 167.

31. Shatzman, "Servants into Planters," p. 215.

32. Data from probate records reported in Table 7, below, describe a similar pattern but suggest that slaves outnumbered servants earlier, in the 1680s, and that blacks were a much larger proportion of the work force in the 1690s. These differences may be a function of the sources. There are few surviving inventories for the Lowcountry before 1720, certainly not enough to support firm conclusions. Further, headright records documents flows, probates stocks: since slaves served for life there should be relatively more of them than short-term servants in inventories. Nevertheless, the differences between Tables 2 and 7 make it clear that we can not yet describe the changing composition of the Lowcountry work force with precision.

33. Wood, *Black Majority*, p. 23.

34. Wilson, *Account of the Province of Carolina*, in Salley, ed., *Narratives*, p. 172.

35. See below and David W. Galenson, *Traders, Planters, and Slaves, Market Behavior in Early English America* (New York, Cambridge University Press, 1986), pp. 1–28.

36. Russell R. Menard, "From Servants to Slaves: The Transformation of the Chesapeake Labor System," *Southern Studies*, 16 (Winter 1977):355–390.

37. For the argument that the transition from servants to slaves in the Lowcountry resembled the process in the West Indies rather than the Chesapeake see David W. Galenson, "Labor Market Behavior in Colonial America" (paper presented to the American Economic Association, New Orleans, 1986), p. 25; and Galenson, *White Servitude in Colonial America*, pp. 154–156.

38. Menard, "Servants to Slaves," p. 366.

39. On the growth rate see Wood, "'More Like a Negro Country.'" Wood accepts the reported import figures and the high rate of increase, arguing that the rise of rice culture and the Africanization of Carolina society turned a slave population that had grown rapidly by reproductive means in the 1710s to one that suffered a reproductive deficit by the 1730s. I agree with Wood's description of trends but think him optimistic regarding the demography of slavery before ca. 1720.

On the beginnings of the African trade see the materials assembled in Elizabeth Donnan, ed., *Documents Illustrative of the History of the Slave Trade to America* (Washington, D.C., Carnegie Institution of Washington, 1930–1935), vol. 4, 235ff., and her essay, "The Slave Trade into South Carolina before the Revolution," *American Historical Review*, 33 (July 1928):804–828.

40. Alexander Hewatt, *An Historical Account of the Rise and Progress of the Colonies of South Carolina and Georgia*, 2 vols. (London, A. Donaldson, 1779), vol. 1, p. 119; [James Glen], *A Description of South Carolina* (London, R. & J. Dodsley, 1761), p. 87.

Notes

41. The literature on the beginnings of rice cultivation is reported in McCusker and Menard, *Economy of British America*, p. 176n. See especially Wood, *Black Majority*, pp. 55–62, and Daniel C. Littlefield, *Rice and Slaves: Ethnicity and the Slave Trade in Colonial South Carolina* (Baton Rouge, Louisiana State University Press, 1981), pp. 74–114. The best introduction to the colonial rice industry remains Lewis C. Gray, *History of Agriculture in the Southern United States to 1860*, 2 vols. (Washington, D.C., Carnegie Institution of Washington, 1933), vol. 1, pp. 277–290. For export data see U.S. Bureau of the Census, *Historical Statistics of the United States, Colonial Times to 1970* (Washington, D.C., Government Printing Office, 1975), Ser. Z 481–499, vol. 2, pp. 1192–1193.

42. Clarence L. Ver Steeg, *Origins of a Southern Mosaic: Studies in Early Carolina and Georgia* (Athens, University of Georgia Press, 1975), pp. 103–132. On the naval stores industry see McCusker and Menard, *Economy of British America*, pp. 179–180.

43. This paragraph summarizes the results of OLS regression analysis of the relationships between slave imports on the one hand and rice exports, naval stores exports, and the value of exports to England from Carolina on the other. See U.S. Bureau of the Census, *Historical Statistics*, Ser. Z 224, pp. 1176–1177, and Ser. Z 481, p. 1192, and Converse D. Clowse, *Economic Beginnings in Colonial South Carolina, 1670–1730*, (Columbia, University of South Carolina Press, 1971), pp. 256–258.

44. Inventory of the estate of Francis Courage, Aug. 13, 1725, Wills, Inventories and Miscellaneous Records, 1724–1725 (WPA transcripts), pp. 352–354, SCDAH.

45. Inventory of the estate of Francis Holmes, 1729 (?), Wills, Inventories and Miscellaneous Records, vol. 62-A, 1729–1731 (WPA transcripts), pp. 429–441.

46. The calculations assume a slave price of L20 sterling and 1500 to 1800 households. The statements concerning the sources of capital are based on a preliminary analysis of mortgages in the several volumes in the series labeled Records of the Secretary of the Province, SCDAH. For examples of English and West Indian capital see Records of the Secretary, 1714–1717, pp. 17–20, 124–126; Records of the Secretary, 1714–1719, pp. 25–26, 39–40. For similar conclusions on financing the growth of slavery in Jamaica see Nuala Zahedieh, "Trade, Plunder, and Economic Development in Early Jamaica," *Economic History Review*, 2nd Ser., 39 (May 1986):205–222.

47. On farm building see Russell R. Menard, Lois Green Carr, and Lorena S. Walsh, "A Small Planter's Profits: The Cole Estate and the Growth of the Early Chesapeake Economy," *William and Mary Quarterly*, 3rd Ser., 40 (April 1983):171–196. There are helpful discussions of the farm-building process and its connection to the growth of slavery in Hewatt, *An Historical Account*, vol. 2, pp. 127–130, 182–183, and David Ramsay, *History of South Carolina from Its First Settlement in 1670 to the Year 1808*, (Newberry, South Carolina, W. J. Duffie, 1858, Spartanburg, South Carolina, Reprint Co., 1959–60), vol. 1, pp. 114–117, which are the sources of the quotations.

48. On the decline of servant migration to Barbados see Galenson, *White Servitude*, p. 82.

49. Harry J. Carman, ed., *American Husbandry* (New York, Columbia University Press, 1939), p. 277. On the transformation produced by the rapid expansion of export agriculture see McCusker and Menard, *Economy of British America*, pp. 181–184.

50. Charles Pinckey as quoted in the *Charleston Evening Gazette*, (28 September 1785). The place of such notions in the ideology of the great planters is

explored in Menard, "Slavery, Economic Growth, and Revolutionary Ideology in the South Carolina Lowcountry."

51. Hewatt, *An Historical Account*, vol. 1, p. 120. On the Georgia debate see Betty Wood, *Slavery in Colonial Georgia, 1730–1775* (Athens, University of Georgia Press, 1984); Ralph Gray and Betty Wood, "The Transition from Indentured to Involuntary Slavery in Colonial Georgia," *Explorations in Economic History*, 13 (October 1976):353–370; and Milton L. Ready, *The Castle Builders: Georgia's Economy under the Trustees, 1732–1754* (New York, Arno Press, 1978).

52. For evidence of the West Indian, specifically Barbadian, influence in the development of slavery in South Carolina see M. Eugene Sirmans, "The Legal Status of the Slave in South Carolina, 1670–1740," *Journal of Southern History*, 28 (November 1962):462–466.

53. Galenson, *White Servitude*, pp. 157–160.

54. Wood, *Black Majority*, pp. 103–124, 196–211, 229–233.

55. This is based on an analysis of slave occupations in the probate inventories cited in Table 7. See also Morgan, "Development of Slave Culture in Eighteenth Century Plantation America," p. 104.

56. The best study of Indian slavery in South Carolina is William Robert Snell, "Indian Slavery in Colonial South Carolina, 1671–1795," Ph.D. Dissertation, University of Alabama, 1972. See also Verner W. Crane, *The Southern Frontier, 1670–1732* (Durham, Duke University Press, 1928); John Donald Duncan, "Servitude and Slavery in Colonial South Carolina, 1670–1776," Ph.D. Dissertation, Emory University, 1972; Almon W. Lauber, *Indian Slavery in Colonial Times within the Present Limits of the United States* (New York, Columbia University, 1913); and J. Leitch Wright, Jr., *The Only Land They Knew: The Tragic Story of the American Indians in the Old South* (New York, Free Press, 1981), pp. 102–150.

57. The best study of the impact of the slave trade on native peoples is Richard White, *The Roots of Dependency: Subsistence, Environment, and Social Change among the Choctaws, Pawnees, and Navahos* (Lincoln, University of Nebraska Press, 1983), pp. 34–68.

58. On prices see Snell, "Indian Slavery," pp. 143–147. Wood makes the case the planters preferred blacks to Indians in *Black Majority*, pp. 37–40.

59. Bailyn, *The Peopling of British North America: An Introduction* (New York, Alfred A. Knopf, 1986), pp. 112–131. One does encounter evidence of such a tension, particularly among the Anglican clergy. See, for examples, the reports of Francis Le Jau and Gideon Johnson as quoted in Crane, *Southern Frontier*, p. 152, 179n.

60. Crane, *Southern Frontier*, pp. 162–186, remains the best account of the Yamasee War.

61. Quoted in Donnan, ed., *Documents Illustrative of the Slave Trade*, vol. 1, p. 125n. Current scholarship questions the traditional view that the Dutch played the major role in the early slave trade to Barbados. See Ernst van den Boogaart and Pieter C. Emmer, "The Dutch Participation in the Atlantic Slave Trade, 1596–1650," in Gemery and Hogendorn, eds., *The Uncommon Market*, pp. 371–375. On the growth of slavery in the West Indies see McCusker and Menard, *Economy of British America*, pp. 149–151; Dunn, *Sugar and Slaves*, pp. 67–74; and Galenson, *Traders, Planters, and Slaves*, pp. 1–28.

62. Dunn, *Sugar and Slaves*, p. 234; Kenneth G. Davies, *The Royal African Company* (London, Longmans, Green, 1957), pp. 337, 362. A comparison of Curtin's estimates of British slave imports during the late seventeenth century

with the number of slaves delivered by the Company suggests that interlopers carried about half the Africans brought to the West Indies from 1675 to 1700. Philip D. Curtin, *The Atlantic Slave Trade: A Census* (Madison, University of Wisconsin Press, 1969), pp. 52–64, 88–89, 119.

63. Wood, *Black Majority*, provides an introduction to these issues.

Notes to TALKING WITH INDIANS
by Patricia Galloway

1. Mason Wade, "The French and the Indians," in Howard Peckham and Charles Gibson, eds., *Attitudes of Colonial Powers Toward the American Indian* (Salt Lake City, University of Utah Press, 1969), pp. 61–80.

2. Several books that should be consulted in judging European attitudes toward the Indian are Robert Berkhofer, *The White Man's Indian* (New York, Alfred A. Knopf, 1978); Francis Jennings, *The Invasion of America: Indians, Colonialism, and the Cant of Conquest* (Chapel Hill, University of North Carolina Press, 1975); James Axtell, *The European and the Indian: Essays in the Ethnohistory of Colonial North America* (New York, Oxford University Press, 1981); and Cornelius J. Jaenen, *Friend and Foe* (Toronto, McClelland and Stewart, 1976). Bruce G. Trigger, in his recent *Natives and Newcomers* (Montreal, McGill-Queen's University Press, 1985), has offered an assessment of French-Indian relations in Canada based upon a more nearly even-handed analysis of both cultures: "The French traders were almost certainly no more altruistic or benevolent than their Dutch counterparts in upper New York State. Yet their desire for profitable trade led them to study Indian ways and made them willing to adopt native conventions and become involved in native alliances when it was in their interest to do so. Furthermore, the traders who were the most willing to do these things were the most successful in the long run," p. 341.

3. Jaenen, *Friend and Foe*, pp. 162–165.

4. Quoted in Jaenen, *Friend and Foe*, p. 54, from Reuben G. Thwaites, ed., *The Jesuit Relations and Allied Documents* (New York, Pageant Book Co., 1959) vol. 9, pp. 87–88.

5. Philippe Aries, *Centuries of Childhood: A Social History of Family Life* (New York, Alfred A. Knopf, 1962); James F. Traer, *Marriage and the Family in Eighteenth-Century France* (Ithaca, New York, Cornell University Press, 1980).

6. Aries, *Childhood*, p. 193.

7. Aries, *Childhood*, p. 193.

8. Archives des Colonies, série C13A (hereinafter cited as C13A), vol. 39, pp. 177–180, Indian Harangues, 6/20/1756, signed and sworn by Grevemberg; C13A, 43:239–241, Minutes of a Council with the Choctaw, 11/14/1763, signed and sworn by Favré.

9. C13A, 12:167–169v, Diron to Huché, 7/9/1729 is a parallel text containing Diron's questions to be addressed to the Indians and the Indian replies as reported by Huché.

10. Glenn R. Conrad, "Reluctant Imperialist: France in North America," and James J. Cooke, "France, the New World, and Colonial Expansion," in Patricia K. Galloway, ed., *La Salle and His Legacy* (Jackson, University Press of Mississippi, 1982).

11. Kerlérec: "The true means . . . to preserve this colony for us and to make it flourish is . . . to attach the Indian nations to us." C13A, 40:153v, Memoir on Indians 12/12/1758.

12. Immanuel M. Wallerstein, *The Modern World-System*, vol. 2: *Mercantilism and the Consolidation of the European World-Economy* (New York, Academic Press, 1980). North American Indians were by Wallerstein's definition on the periphery of a periphery: pp. 166–167.

13. Verner W. Crane, *The Southern Frontier, 1670–1732* (Ann Arbor, University of Michigan Press, 1956), pp. 4–5.

14. James Leitch Wright, *The Only Land They Knew* (New York, The Free Press, 1981), pp. 138, 150. Also see William R. Snell, "Indian Slavery in Colonial South Carolina, 1671–1795," Ph.D. Dissertation, University of Alabama, 1972.

15. Patricia K. Galloway, "Henri de Tonti du village des Chacta, 1702," in Galloway, ed., *La Salle and His Legacy*, pp. 146–175.

16. Charles R. Maduell, Jr., *The Census Tables for the French Colony of Louisiana From 1699 Through 1732* (Baltimore, Genealogial Publishing Co., 1972).

17. Pierre Margry, *Découvertes et établissements des français dans l'ouest et dans le sud de l'Amérique Septentrionale (1615–1754)*, (Paris, Impro. D. Jouaust, 1875–86), vol. 4, pp. 43–44, 422, 448, 451, 480, 521.

18. Marcel Giraud, *A History of French Louisiana*, trans. Joseph C. Lambert, vol. 1 (Baton Rouge, Louisiana State University Press, 1974), p. 85.

19. Richebourg Gaillard McWilliams, ed., and trans., *Iberville's Gulf Journals* (University, University of Alabama Press, 1981), pp. 176–177.

20. Richebourg Gaillard McWilliams, *Fleur de Lys and Calumet* (Baton Rouge, Louisiana State University Press, 1953), pp. 73–78.

21. McWilliams, *Gulf Journals*, p. 137.

22. McWilliams, *Fleur de Lys*, pp. 25–30.

23. There is a remote possibility that the Le Vaseur noted as an interpreter to the Alabamas at Fort Toulouse in 1746 may be a son of the boy Pierre LeVasseur; Huntington Manuscript Loudoun 9 (the Vaudreuil Letterbooks, hereinafter cited as HMLO 9), vol. 3:194, Vaudreuil to Le Sueur, 5/?/1746.

24. Giraud, *History*, p. 85.

25. C13A, 2:225–7, 8/12/1708.

26. C13A, 2:183–184, Bienville to Pontchartrain, 10/12/1708.

27. AC, series B. 30:128–129, Pontchartrain to Bienville, 7/11/1709.

28. C13A, 16:31–31v, Salmon to Maurepas, 5/7/1733.

29. C13A, 17:232v, Louboey to Maurepas, 5/8/1733.

30. HMLO 9, III:156, Vaudreuil to D'Erneville, 3/7/1745; 159, Vaudreuil to Hazeur, 6/1/1745.

31. C13C, 1:373v, Bienville's Memoir on Indians, 1726.

32. McWilliams, *Gulf Journals*, pp. 59, 126.

33. James M. Crawford, *The Mobilian Trade Language* (Knoxville, University of Tennessee Press, 1978); McWilliams, *Fleur de Lys*, p. 81.

34. McWilliams, *Gulf Journals*, p. 59.

35. *Journal of Paul Du Ru*, trans., Ruth Lapham Butler (Chicago, The Caxton Club, 1934), p. 8.

36. C13A, 8:404v, Father Raphael to Abbé Raguet, 5/15/1725; C13A, 11:338, Périer and La Chaise to Directors, 4/22/1729.

37. McWilliams, *Fleur de Lys*, pp. 81, 181.

38. *Cf.* C13A, 2:549, Bienville to Pontchartrain, 6/21/1710.

39. HMLO 9, III:74, Vaudreuil to La Houssaye, 4/22/1744; 16, Vaudreuil to La Houssaye, 11/21/1743.

40. Wilbur Jacobs, *Wilderness Politics and Indian Gifts: The Northern Colonial Frontier, 1748–1763* (Lincoln, University of Nebraska Press, 1966), pp. 11–45.

41. Initially, Bienville hoped to present a large quantity of French goods as a present to the French-approved Great Chief of a tribe, with the idea that he would redistribute the goods to those Indians who adhered to the French line; thus the power of pro-French chiefs would be enhanced. As time passed this initial design was diluted, so that a hierarchy of presents was instituted, with lesser chiefs and even warriors who had performed specific deeds being rewarded directly by the French; this practice operated to undermine the power of pro-French chiefs. C13A, 16:207–208v, Bienville Memoir on Indians, 1733.

42. Bienville was only the first of the governors of Louisiana to be accused of keeping and profiting from these Indian presents. C13A, 2:249–312, Abstract of Testimony, 2/24–27/1708.

43. C13A, 39:177, Indian Harangues, 6/20/1756.

44. C13A, 43:244, Minutes of a Council with the Choctaw, 11/14/1763.

45. HMLO 9, III.

46. C13A, 4:766v, Bienville to Pontchartrain, 1/2/1716.

47. C13A, 12:74–77, Régis du Roullet Journal, 1729.

48. C13A, 35:368, Bobé Descloseaux to Rouillé, 4/21/1767.

49. C13A, 7:119, 124, Superior Council Minutes, 5/16–10/13/1723.

50. HMLO 9, III:63, Vaudreuil to Develle, 2/29/1744.

51. C13A, 21:184v, Bienville to Maurepas, 6/29/1736.

52. C13A, 22:98v–99, Bienville to Maurepas, 6/17/1737.

53. C13A, 10:139v, Dodun memoir, 1726.

54. C13A, 14:184v, Bienville to Salmon, 11/23/1732.

55. *Cf.* C13A, 21: 195, Bienville to Maurepas, 6/28/1736, which mentions on interpreter's being left behind at a river crossing with pirogues to help the Choctaws cross and lead them to the rendezvous.

56. C13A, 21:184v, Bienville to Maurepas, 6/29/1736.

57. C13A, 27:66, Bienville to Maurepas, 3/28/1742.

58. HMLO 9, III: 156, Vaudreuil to d'Erneville, 3/7/1745.

59. C13A, 12:373v, Diron d'Artaguette to Maurepas, 3/29/1730.

60. C13A, 12:65–66, Périer to Régis du Roullet, 8/21/1729.

61. This can be inferred from the results of the tests to which he was put, attempting to converse with two groups of Choctaw: C13A, 12:22, Régis du Roullet Journal, 1729.

62. C13A, 15:197–211v, Régis du Roullet to Maurepas, 1729–33; C13A, 12:100–134v, Lusser's Journal, 1730.

63. C13A, 12: 130v–131, Lusser's Journal, 1730; C13A, 15:200, Régis du Roullet to Maurepas, 1729.

64. C13A, 12:104v, Lusser's Journal, 1730.

65. HMLO 9, III:207, Vaudreuil to Louboey, 8/28/1746; 212, Vaudreuil to Hazeur, 8/28/1746; 213, Vaudreuil to Beauchamp, 8/28/1746.

66. *Cf.* C13A, 17:39–41, Salmon to Maurepas, 2/8/1733.

67. HMLO 9, III:38, 1/5/1744; 55, 1/1/1744.

68. HMLO 9, III:71, Vaudreuil to La Houssaye, 4/11/1744.

69. C13A, 12:167–69v, Diron d'Artaguette to Huché.

70. C13A, 10:139v, Dodun Memoir, 1726.

71. *Cf.* C13A, 29:194v, Louboey to Maurepas, 10/6/1745.

72. C13A, 12:110v, Lusser's Journal, 1730.

73. C13A, 14:12v, Benoît to Périer, 3/29/1732.

74. HMLO 9, III:253, Vaudreuil to Louboey, 2/24/1747.

75. C13A, 21:135, Bienville to Maurepas, 2/10/1736.

76. *Cf.* Patricia K. Galloway, "Louisiana Post Letters," *Louisiana History*, 22 (Winter 1981): 31–44.

77. C13A, 12:67–99, Régis du Roullet Journal, 1729; C13A, 12:100–134v, Lusser's Journal, 1730; C13A, 15:197–211, Régis du Roullet to Maurepas, 1729–33.

78. C13A, 15:209v–210, Régis du Roullet to Maurepas, 1732.

79. C13A, 30:169v, Louboey to Maurepas, 2/8/1746.

80. C13A, 12:125v, Lusser's Journal, 1730. It is possible that this boy was the same young Massé whose aptitude for "Mobilian" made Louboey recommend him as an interpreter trainee later; see note 29.

81. Patricia K. Galloway, "The Chief who is Your Father: Choctaw and French Views of the Diplomatic Relation," in press.

82. AC, B, 29:256, Louis XIV to de Muy, 6/3/1707; C13A, 2:423v–424, Bienville to Pontchartrain, 8/12 and 9/1/1709.

83. Samuel Wells, "The Role of Mixed-Bloods in Mississippi Choctaw History," in Samuel J. Wells and Roseanna Tubby, eds., *After Removal: The Choctaw in Mississippi* (Jackson, University Press of Mississippi, 1986), pp. 42–55.

84. Favré was interpreter for the King in Mobile at the cession to England in 1763 and continued in the service of the English, Spanish, and American governments that followed, founding a white lumber barony on the lower Pearl river. See John H. Napier, *Lower Pearl River's Piney Woods: Its Land and People* (University, Miss., Center for the Study of Southern Culture, 1985), p. 208, n. 73.

85. HMLO 9, III:135, Vaudreuil to Baudouin, 9/28/1744.

86. C13A, 13:177v–178, Régis du Roullet to Périer, 2/1/1731; C13A, 14:190v–191, Baudouin to Salmon, 11/23/1732.

87. HMLO 9, III:182, Vaudreuil to Louboey, 10/13/1745; 271, Vaudreuil to Louboey, 7/30/1747.

88. C13A, 13:177v, 178, Régis du Roullet to Périer, 2/1/1731.

89. Jacqueline Olivier Vidrine, *Love's Legacy: The Mobile Marriages Recorded in French, Transcribed, with Annotated Abstracts in English, 1724–1786* (Lafayette, Center for Louisiana Studies, 1985) constitutes a record of intimate social gatherings that shows the interactions of the various circles of Mobile society through the period, since each marriage is witnessed by those who attended.

90. C13A, 6:146v–147, Council Minutes, 2/18/1721.

91. AC, G1, 464, 1721 and 1726 censuses; AC, F1, 13:113, 1706 census.

92. The inference is based upon Huché's disappearance from both the documents and the marriage records around this time.

93. C13A, 29:194v, Louboey to Maurepas, 10/16/1745, calls him "a prudent and sensible lad . . . brought up among them and has a perfect command of the language."

Notes to THE SOUTHERN COLONIES: A GENERAL PERSPECTIVE
by Robert Middlekauff

1. (Chapel Hill, University of North Carolina Press, 1985).

2. Jack P. Greene, ed., *The Diary of Colonel Landon Carter of Sabine Hall,*

1752–1778, 2 vols. (Charlottesville, University Press of Virginia, 1965), pp. 20, 245–246, 379, 383, 630, 755–756, 990–991, *passim*.

3. David S. Lovejoy, *Religious Enthusiasm in the New World: Heresy to Revolution* (Cambridge, Harvard University Press, 1985); Philip Gura, *A Glimpse of Sion's Glory* (Middletown, Connecticut, Wesleyan University Press, 1984).

4. Rhys Isaac, *The Transformation of Virginia, 1740–1790* (Chapel Hill, University of North Carolina Press, 1982).

5. (Chapel Hill, University of North Carolina Press, 1968). See also David Brion Davis, *The Problem of Slavery in Western Culture* (Ithaca, New York, Cornell University Press, 1966); and Orlando Patterson, *Slavery and Social Death: A Comparative Study* (Cambridge, Mass., Harvard University Press, 1982).

6. (New York, W. W. Norton, 1975).

Contributors

Thad W. Tate received his Ph. D. in History at Brown University in 1960. His many articles in the history of the colonial south have brought him a great deal of recognition in the field as has his monograph, *The Negro in Eighteenth Century America* (University Press of Virginia, 1966). He was a Fellow in the American Council of Learned Societies from 1970 to 1971, and is currently the Director of the Institute of Early American History and Culture.

Daniel Blake Smith received his Ph. D. from the University of Virginia in 1978. His book, *Inside the Great House: Planters Life in Eighteenth Century Chesapeake Society* was published by Cornell University Press in 1980. His numerous articles have appeared in historical and psychological journals, revealing his strong commitment to an interdisciplinary approach to the study of family history.

Patricia K. Galloway received her Ph. D. in Comparative Literature in 1973 at the University of North Carolina. Currently working in the Mississippi Department of Archives and History, she has published a vast number of articles in the fields of archeology, history, language and literature. She has also edited *LaSalle and His Legacy: Frenchmen and Indians in the Lower Mississippi Valley* (University Press of Mississippi, 1982).

Russell R. Menard received his Ph. D. in History in 1975 from the University of Iowa. From 1974 to 1976 he was a Research Fellow at the Institute of Early American History and Culture. His research in Maryland History, and particularly his studies in American slavery, are among the best works of their kind in the field. His book, *Economy and Society in Early Colonial Maryland*, was published by Garland Press in 1985.

Philip D. Morgan received his Ph. D. in History at University College, London in 1978. His articles and books are well-known for their analyses of the slave experience in the colonial South. His most recent book, *Slave Counterpoint: Black Culture in the Eighteenth Century Chesapeake and Lowcountry*, is being published by the Institute of Early American History and Culture.

Robert Middlekauff received his Ph. D. in History at Yale University. A recipient of the Bancroft Prize in American History and Culture, he is well-known for his research in colonial America. He has published numerous books and articles dealing with both seventeenth and eighteenth century topics. His most recent book, *the Glorious Cause: The American Revolution, 1760–89* (Oxford University Press), received the Faunces Tavern Museum Book Award in 1982.

Winthrop D. Jordan received his Ph.D. in History at Brown University in 1960. His seminal work, *White Over Black: American Attitudes Toward the Negro, 1550–1812* (Institute of Early American History and Culture, 1968), received the Parkman Prize, the National Book Award and the Bancroft Prize. He is the author of numerous articles dealing with topics in American colonial history and Black history, and is currently working on a study of an abortive slave uprising in Adams County, Mississippi.

Sheila L. Skemp received her Ph.D. in History at the University of Iowa in 1974. She has written articles on colonial Newport, Rhode Island, and co-edited a monograph, *Race, Sex and the Role of Women in the South*. She is now working on a biography of William Franklin, loyalist son of Benjamin Franklin and the last colonial governor of New Jersey.

Index

169

Index